Allensworth

A Place. A People. A Story.

August 16, 2010 – February 27, 2011
California African American Museum

CALIFORNIA AFRICAN AMERICAN MUSEUM

First edition
10 9 8 7 6 5 4 3 2 1
ISBN: 978-0-9789818-8-4
Library of Congress Control Number 2011928222

California African American Museum
600 State Drive, Exposition Park, Los Angeles, CA 90037
A California State Museum, Jerry Brown, Governor

Cover and title page photo by Ted Dayton.

Foreword

I don't recall how I first learned about Colonel Allensworth State Historic Park ("Allensworth"), but since first reading about it a few years ago, I knew that I wanted to visit. Finally, returning early from a trip photographing in Yosemite Valley, I decided to visit Allensworth. Luckily my visit coincided with one of the five days annually in which the Friends of Allensworth hold a special event. The special event consisted of tours of most of the structures, lead by members of the Friends of Allensworth. The docents provided the history of the structure they were showing and answered any and all questions. They even allowed me to set up my camera and tripod to take photos of the buildings.

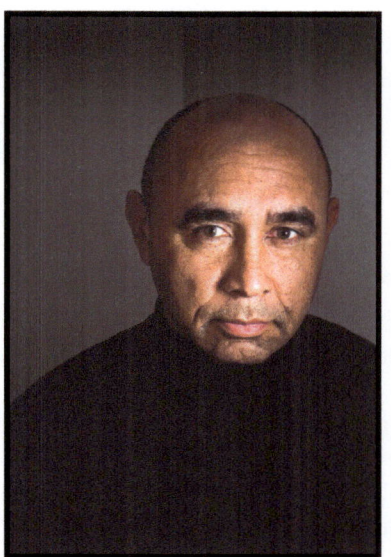

I was enthralled by the living history of Allensworth, but surprised that there were so few visitors present during my visit. I even recall one of the docents commenting that there seemed to be more docents in the park that day than visitors. As I returned home that day, I was determined to figure out a means that I could somehow, in some small way, do something to assist in keeping the vision of the founders of Allensworth alive.

The State of California has many little known treasures, of which Allensworth is one. Although my efforts as a single individual were unlikely to positively impact Allensworth, I knew that if I could figure out a way to leverage my efforts, and that of others, we could perhaps make a difference. That is how this book, "The Allensworth Project" was born.

The idea I came up with was to let loose upon Allensworth a group of talented, award winning photographers, all of whom view the world differently, to come up with a collection of photographs that capture the essence of Allensworth. Upon arriving home from Allensworth, I began contacting fellow members of the Santa Clarita Valley Photographers Association with the idea that each photographer would contribute his or her images for inclusion in a book. Our collective work could then be donated with all benefits from the sale of the book going to the Friends of Allensworth.

If you've visited Allensworth you will not be surprised to learn that each of the photographers involved in "The Allensworth Project" fell in love with Allensworth the day we photographed it. Hopefully you will find that our photographs reflect the history and spirit of one of the hidden gems of California.

- Rick Russell, Santa Clarita

3

The California African American Museum's Passion for Allensworth

There are historians and scholars who decry the absence of any mention of Allensworth in American History books. Perhaps it is just one sociologically scarring element in the litany of African American achievements that have never received proper status in the telling of events in our nation's history. Perhaps that is why since 1984, the year the California African American Museum (CAAM) opened at its current location[1], we have felt the urgency of presenting the history of Allensworth to our patrons as it poignantly fulfills our cultural mission of presenting for public enrichment the wonders of African American contributions in our great state of California. It is genuinely historic that Allensworth became California's first Black-founded, financed and governed town in 1908.

We have interpreted the art and culture of this monumental achievement through a variety of different exhibits: in 1987, *Allensworth: An Enduring Dream*, curated by CAAM's former history curator Lonnie Bunch, opened its doors presenting vintage photographs, documents and artifacts gathered from collections of former residents and complemented by ephemera from private and State archives.

In 2008, *Allensworth: 100 Years of the California Dream*, revisited Allensworth in its centenary, placing the town within a rich and dense historical content, including video segments. This exhibition, guest curated by Susan Anderson and CAAM's former history curator Christopher Jimenez y West, was supported by local politicians — among them, Mark Ridley Thomas, who made it possible for the show to travel widely throughout the State.

In fall 2010, we gained another opportunity to share Allensworth with the world when photographer Rick Russell approached our visual arts curator Mar Hollingsworth with a visually stunning and lesser-known side of Allensworth: contemporary, full-color photographs taken by a multicultural group of artists who had been captivated by the charm of the town and were determined to do what they could to preserve its legacy. This time, *Allensworth: A Place. A People. A Story.* offered the immediacy of an environment that remains alive thanks to the efforts of the many people who continue to value the history of African Americans in California.

As we looked at Allensworth through this new lens, we also looked back to note the story of what was first referred to as the Allensworth Colony and its founder Allen Allensworth. He was born into slavery, escaped during the Civil War and served with the Union Army. After the war he and his brother operated two highly successful restaurants in St. Louis, while Allen also managed to continue his formal education. In 1871 he became a minister, and in 1877 he met and married Josephine Leavel, a young schoolteacher and talented pianist and organist. In 1886, Allensworth accepted a commission in the Army as a Chaplain to serve in the all-Black 24th Army Infantry. When Allensworth retired in 1906, he held the rank of lieutenant colonel

---

[1] The California African American Museum ("CAAM") was enacted after a finding by the Legislature that *"there is a need for a state repository dedicated to the diverse contributions of Afro-Americans to the history and culture of this state and the nation."* Out of Assembly Bill No. 420, Chapter 571, the Museum was chartered September 1977 by the State of California under the California Food and Agriculture Code 4104, as the California Museum of Afro-American History and Culture. The name changed to the California Afro-American Museum and then again to its current namesake: the California African American Museum. For the first seven years, CAAM was housed and hosted exhibitions inside its sister agency the California Museum of Science and Industry, now known as the California Science Center.

and was not only the highest-ranking Chaplain in the Army, but the highest-ranking Black officer of this time.

After his retirement from the Army, Colonel Allensworth, Professor William Payne, and three other Black men decided to establish a self-governed town for Black people. They envisioned a place where Blacks could own property and achieve their full economic potential free from the discriminatory laws and practices that plagued Blacks throughout the country.

The site finally chosen for their colony was midway between Los Angeles and San Francisco— along the Santa Fe Railroad line about nine miles east of Earlimart in the southwest corner of Tulare County. They invited 42 select settlers to begin this colony. Of those, 37 showed up.

There was plenty of inexpensive farmland and several artesian wells. The new town grew rapidly as enterprising Black men and women—nurses, business owners, educators, farmers, ranchers, retired soldiers and crafts people—purchased town lots, started farms and built homes. It was not long until the prospering town had a school, church, library, and post office. Allensworth's businesses included a hotel, machine shop, bakery, drug store, and barbershop.

In its heyday, Allensworth bustled with activity. The town was a railroad transfer point, providing a steady stream of customers for Allensworth's many businesses. The grain and cattle merchants of Allensworth used the railroad to move their products to market. While the town's shops and stores supplied day-to-day needs for living, the church and school provided for the spiritual and educational needs of the town's people. The women of Allensworth organized formal debates, concerts, plays, club meetings and other social activities that brought people together transforming the town into a closely-knit community.

Allensworth's streets were all named after noted African-Americans—abolitionists Sojourner Truth and Frederick Douglass, Col. Charles Young, poet Paul Lawrence Dunbar—abolitionists—Harriet Beecher Stowe—and supporters of Allensworth—David Palmer.

Allensworth flourished until Col. Allensworth was killed in 1914 when he was run over by two motorcyclists in Monrovia. The death was not without rumor and speculation that the accident was intentional, meant to derail the flourishing community, but no such conspiracy was ever proven.

Other factors also impacted Allensworth's survivability. Water that was readily available in the early years began to diminish as farming demands up stream and deep well pumping throughout the San Joaquin Valley lowered the natural sources of water available to the people of Allensworth. The growth of trucking also began to replace trains as a source of transporting farm products, causing many in Allensworth in the '20s and '30s to seek work elsewhere. The need for drafted and enlisted men during World War II also took its toll. Allensworth remained the home to a handful of families and individuals throughout the 20th century, but eventually, the town went into such a decline that by the 60s, almost nothing was left of people or property.

In the wake of the assassination of Dr. Martin Luther King, Jr., an employee of California's Department of Parks and Recreation named Ed Pope felt compelled to do something. "I remembered Col. Allensworth and the town he founded," Pope recalled to the *Visalia Times-Delta* on January 17, 2004. Interest in restoring Allensworth was further kindled by an *Ebony* magazine article in September 1966 entitled, "The Town That Refused to Die." With the help of a professor at California State University, Pope wrote a proposal to restore the Allensworth settlement as a state historical site and pitched it to the Parks Department. Finally, in 1974, Gov. Ronald Reagan authorized the department to establish the park. Col. Allensworth Historic State Park was established on 240 acres in 1976.

The state parks department has since built more than 15 buildings on the original site of the colony as duplicates of the original Allensworth buildings, including a school, church, store, meeting center and the houses of many of the colony's prominent citizens, including Col. Allensworth, the Stocktons, Hacketts and Dodsons. No structure is permitted to be built at Allensworth Park that cannot be documented as existing there between 1908 and 1920.

Colonel Allen Allensworth's dream is recreated and maintained daily by those who painstakingly work to keep the environment of Allensworth alive. The settlement reconstruction is the subject of the exhibition of contemporary photographs in *Allensworth: A Place. A People. A Story.* The power and beauty of these extraordinarily vibrant photographs give the viewer a sense of actually being in the Allensworth site. In addition to recognizing the historic significance of Allensworth, these images are also personalized interpretations by photographic artists Rick Russell, David Paul Green, Mel and Karen Carll, Clark Campbell, Jean Carter, Ted Dayton, Christy Stallcup, Robert Mance and April Bielefeldt; all of whom sought to recreate the soul of that pioneering spirit through their modern camera lenses.

Conceived as a photographic study by Russell, the result is a collective effort by the photographers. The actual images on the exhibition were printed by Mel Carll of the SCV Center for Photography, and the organization of the photographs into an exhibition was project managed by CAAM visual arts curator Mar Hollingsworth. The exhibition includes a video created by Dusty and Barbara Stiles that celebrates the contributions of today's docents and volunteers to sustaining the stories and the place that became Allensworth.

We admire each photographer for not only finding a way to capture the essence of Colonel Allensworth's vision, but for wanting to share what a tremendously breathtaking place Allensworth continues to be. We are also very grateful for the generosity of their collective efforts in donating their images to CAAM's permanent collection. It is efforts such as this that allow the California African American Museum to fulfill our mission to research, collect, preserve and interpret for public enrichment the history, art and culture of African Americans with an emphasis on California and the Western United States. Welcome to *Allensworth: A Place. A People. A Story.*

Charmaine Jefferson, Executive Director, California African American Museum

To learn more about Allensworth Historic State Park, to visit, and/or join in supporting its continued preservation, we recommend contacting the following organizations for the latest information:

California State Parks
http://www.parks.ca.gov/?page_id=583

The Friends of Allensworth Cooperating Association
http://www.friendsofallensworth.com/allensworth/allensworth_history.html

Friends of Allensworth San Diego Chapter
http://friendsofallensworthsandiego.com/about.htm

Out in the Middle of Somewhere

From the California State Parks website:

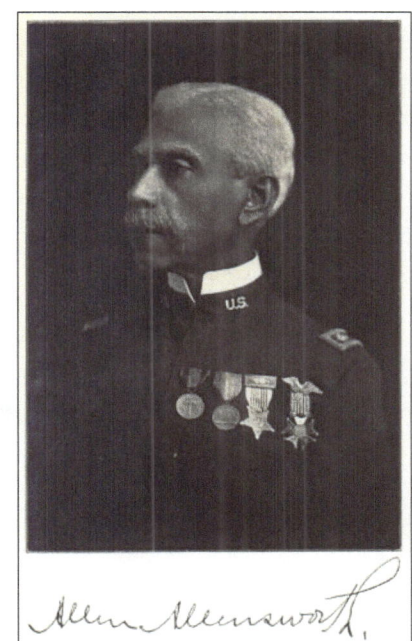

Allen Allensworth was born a slave in Louisville, Kentucky, in 1842. At the age of 12, he was "sold down river" for trying to learn to read and write. After some trading by slave dealers, he was taken to New Orleans, and bought by a slaveholder to become a jockey. The Civil War started, and when the Union forces neared Louisville, Allensworth found his chance for freedom. He joined the Navy and when he was discharged, he had achieved the rank of first class petty officer. In 1871, he was ordained as a Baptist minister and entered the Baptist Theological Institute at Nashville. While serving at the Union Baptist Church in Cincinnati, he learned of the need for African American chaplains in the armed services, and got an appointment as Chaplain of the 24th Infantry.

He had seen many African Americans move west after the Civil War to escape discrimination. With four other men with similar vision, Allensworth decided to establish a place where African Americans could live and thrive without oppression. On June 30, 1908, they formed the California Colony Home Promoting Association. They selected an area in Tulare County because it was fertile, there was plenty of water, and the land was available and inexpensive. They first bought 20 acres, and later, 80 more. The little

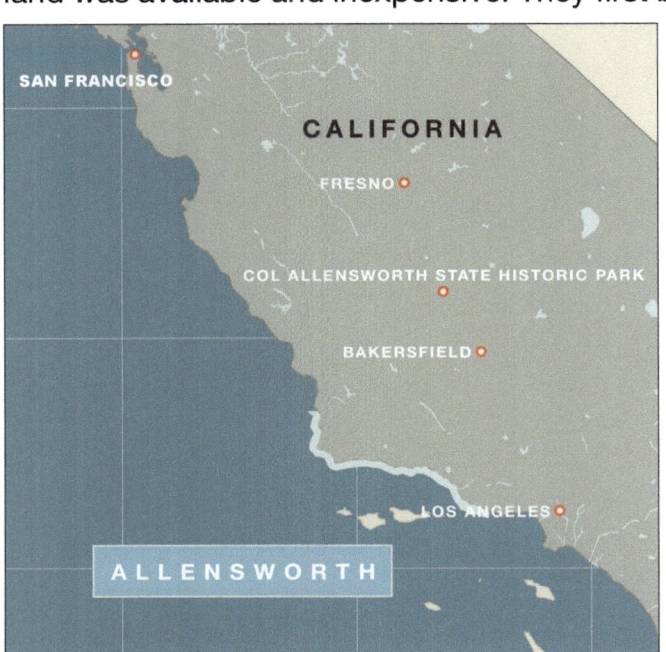

town with a big vision grew rapidly forseveral years -- to more than 200 inhabitants, by 1914. That same year Allensworth became a voting precinct and a judicial district. Colonel Allensworth was killed on September 14, 1914, when hit by a motorcycle, while getting off a streetcar in Monrovia. After a funeral at the Second Baptist Church in Los Angeles, he was buried with full military honors.

Since most of the water for Allensworth farming had to come underground from the Sierra Nevada mountains, and there were many other farms and communities between the mountains and Allensworth, the water supply for the town and farms began to dry up. The next blow was the Great Depression that hit the whole country in the early 1930s. Public services began to shut down, and many residents moved to the cities to look for work. The Post Office closed in

continued next page

1931. By the 1940s, most of the residents were migratory farm workers, and the population was mainly a mixture of Blacks and Hispanics. Housing deteriorated, as most of the people didn't consider Allensworth their permanent home. The population had shrunk to 90, in 1972, and later dropped to almost zero.

A drive began in the early 1970s to save the town of Allensworth. Allensworth would be an historic monument and public park dedicated to the memory and spirit of Colonel Allensworth as well as a place to note the achievements and contributions of African Americans to the history and development of California. In 1976, when the town site became a state historic park, restorations began, and plans began for further preservation, restoration, and reconstruction, and for interpretation of the history of Allensworth.

★★★

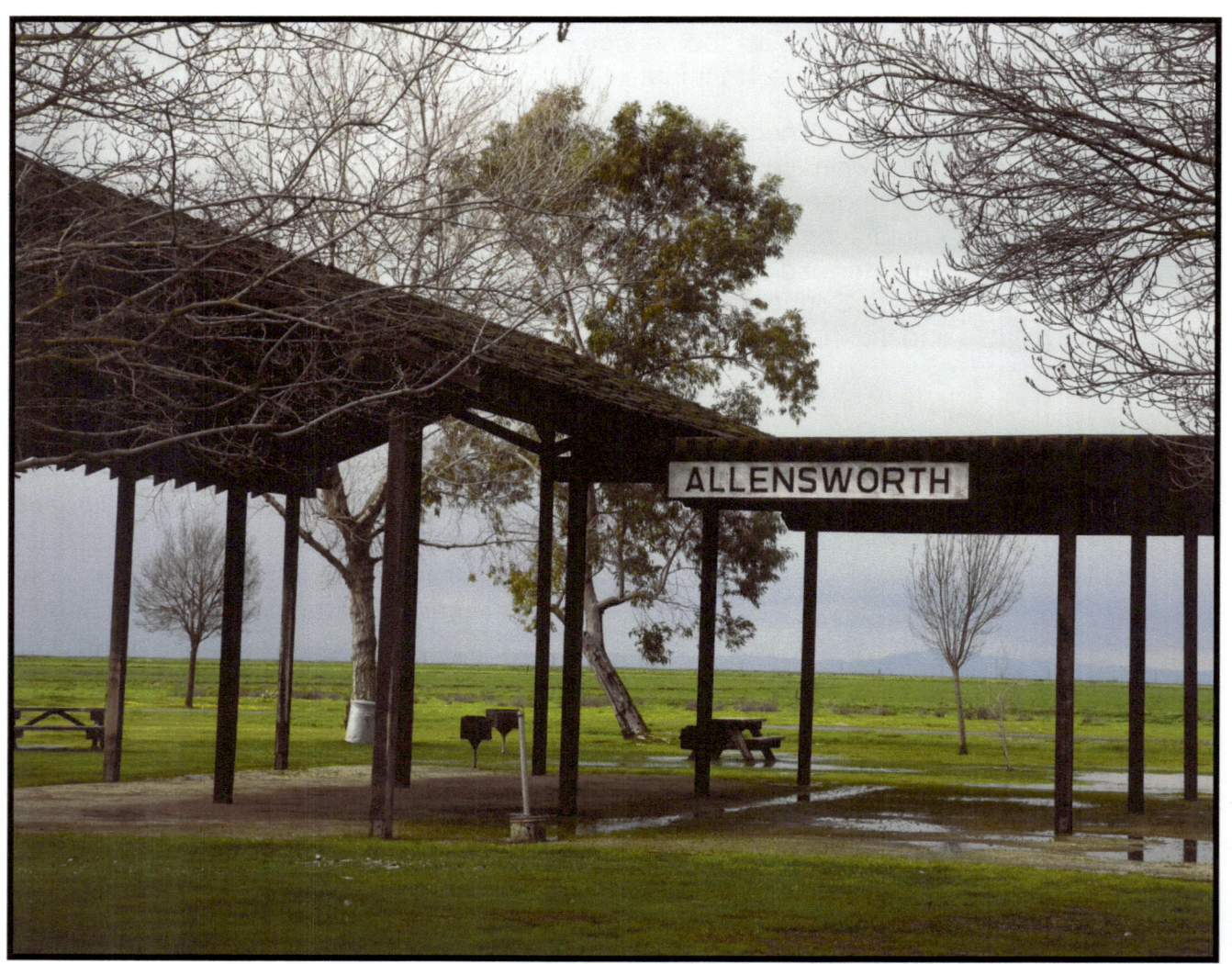

Allensworth - Jean Carter

"Sign on the protective shelter over the day use area located by the visitor's center. The shelter provides protection from the elements and is a nice place to picnic for visitors."

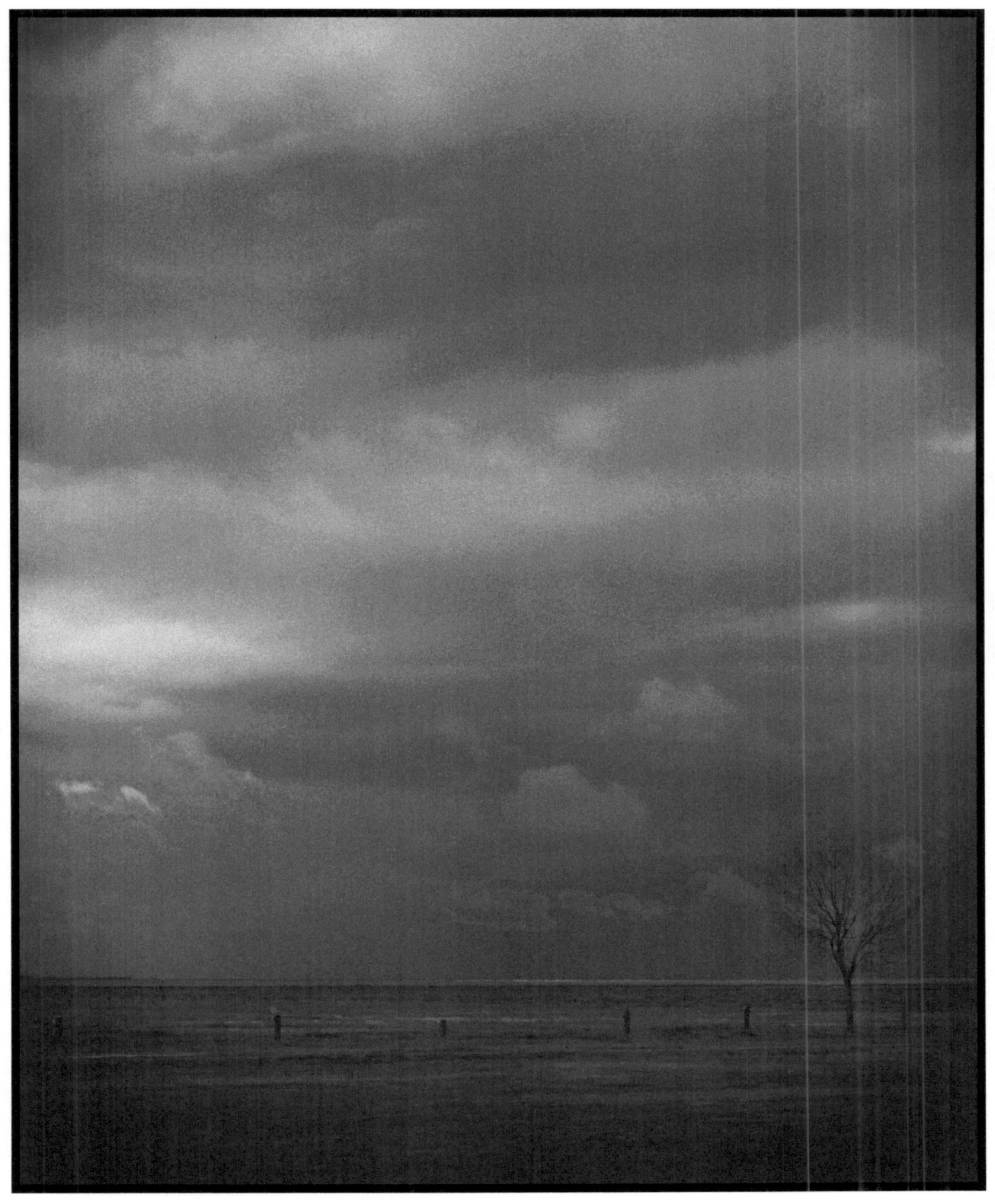

Blustery Nothingness - Clark Campbell

"View of the surrounding terrain looking southwest past the Schoolhouse at Allensworth State Historic Park."

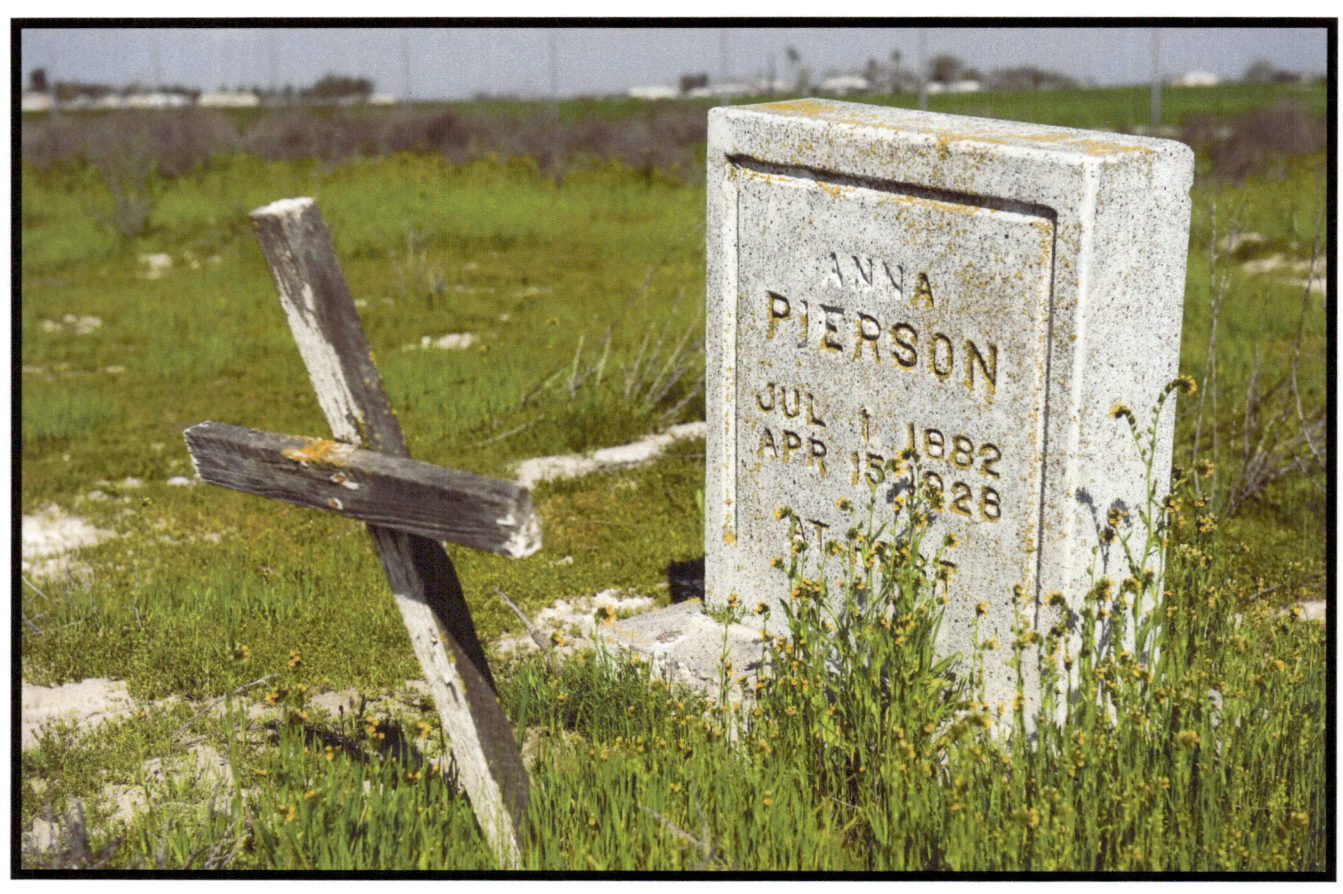

Anna Pierson – Allensworth Cemetery - Christy Stallcup

"A headstone marks the grave of Anna Pierson, which is located in the Allensworth Historical Cemetery."

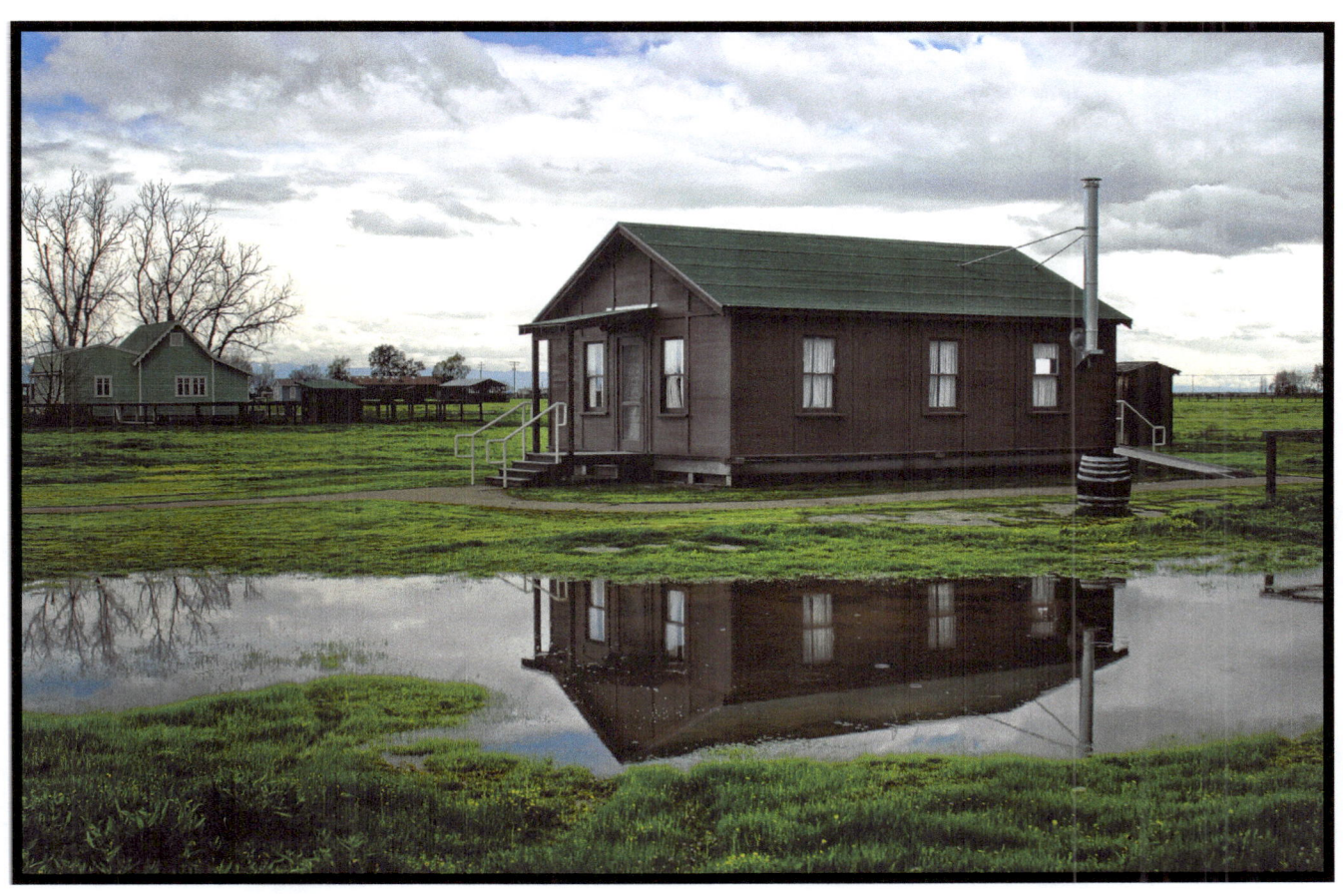

Phillips House - Robert Mance

"Sergeant James Phillips house reflected in a pond on a stormy day."

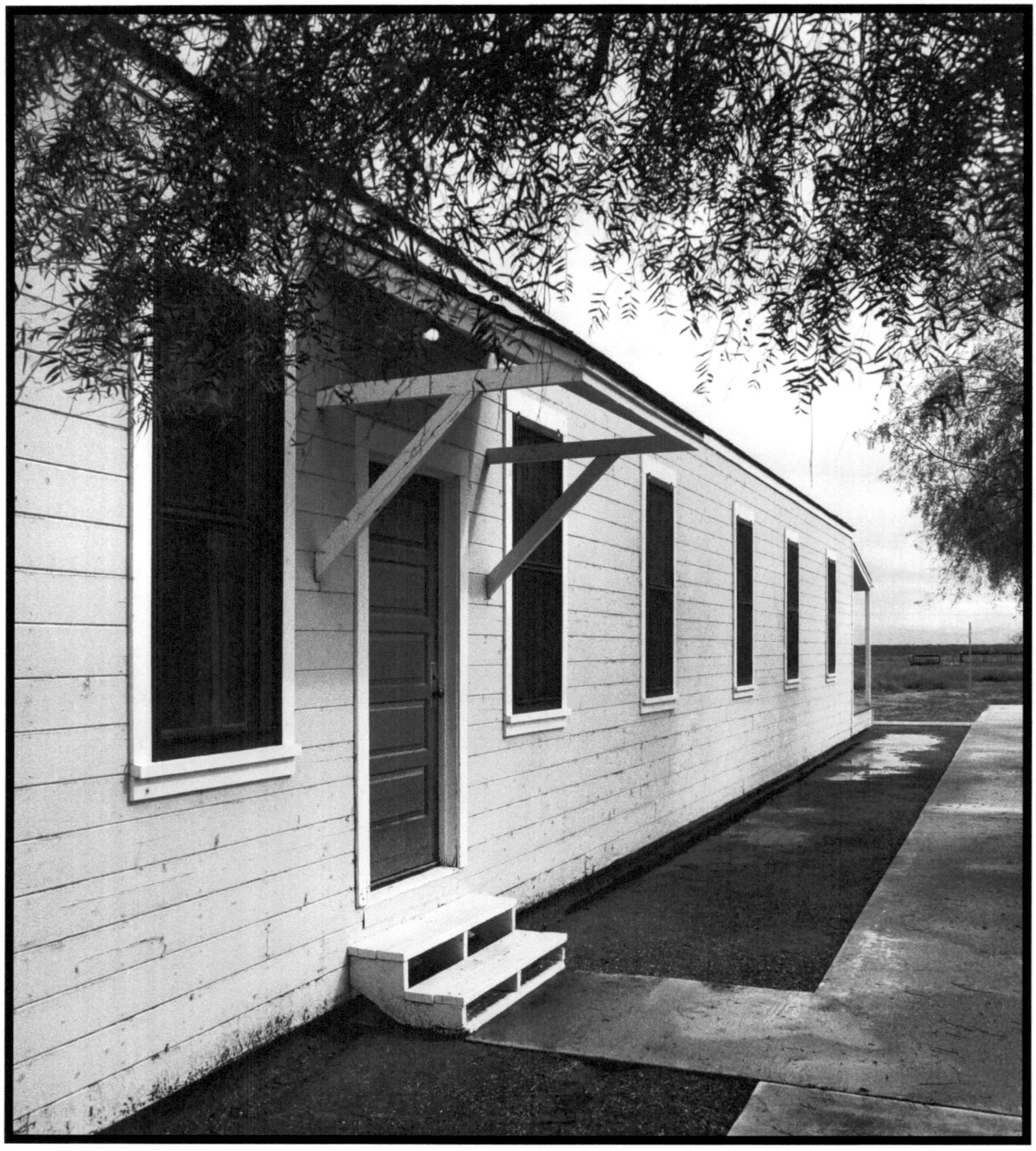

Allensworth Hotel, Side View - Ted Dayton

"The Allensworth Hotel, opened in 1910, is on the north side of town, on Palmer Avenue. While the formal entrance to the hotel faces east, this view of the hotel shows the south side, facing toward Palmer. Directly across the street is Frank Milner's barbershop, no doubt the social center for the men of Allensworth."

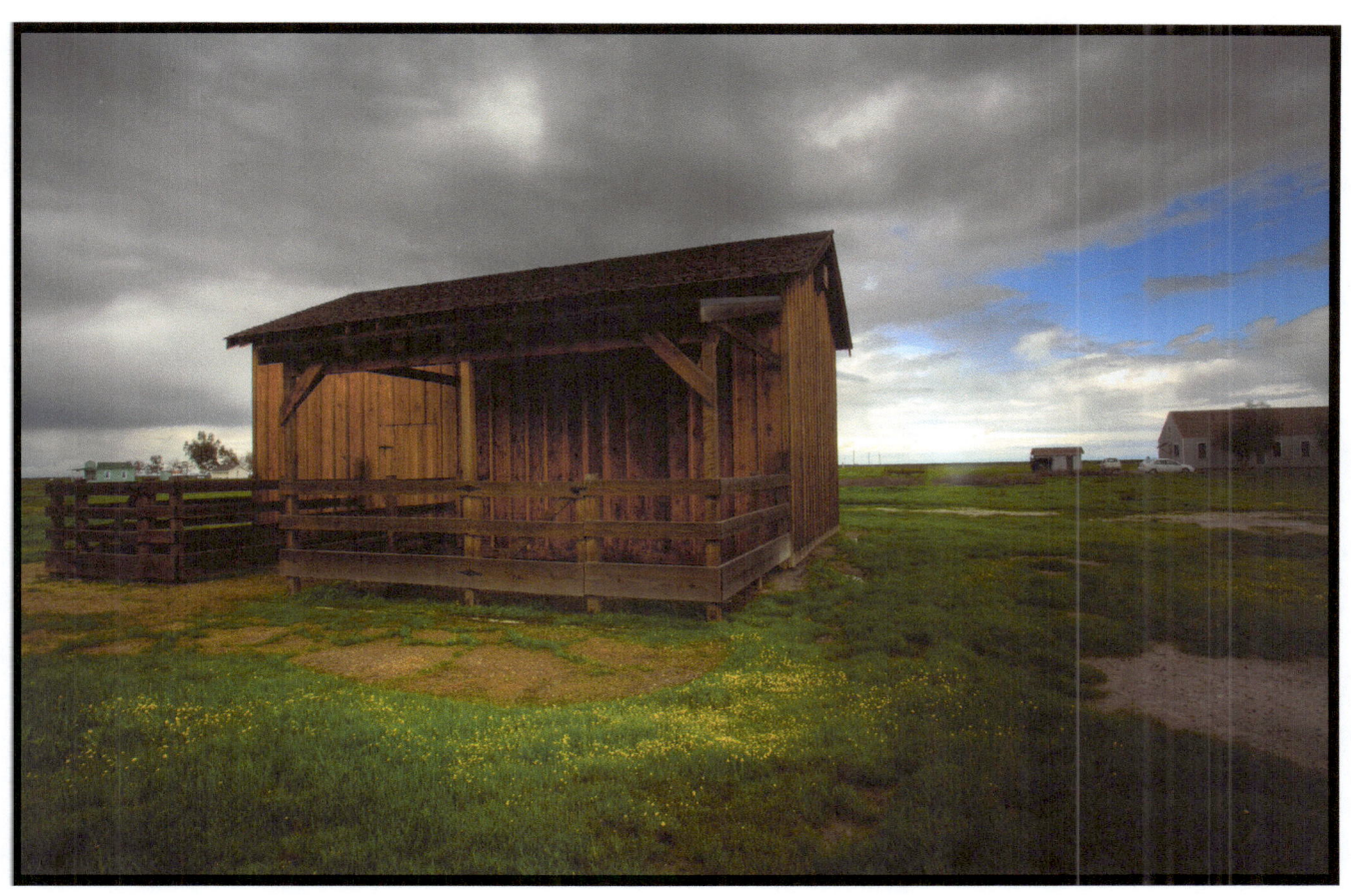

Smattering of Wildflowers - David Paul Green

"In such harsh conditions, the intense colors of even a small sprinkling of yellow flowers create a joyous riot."

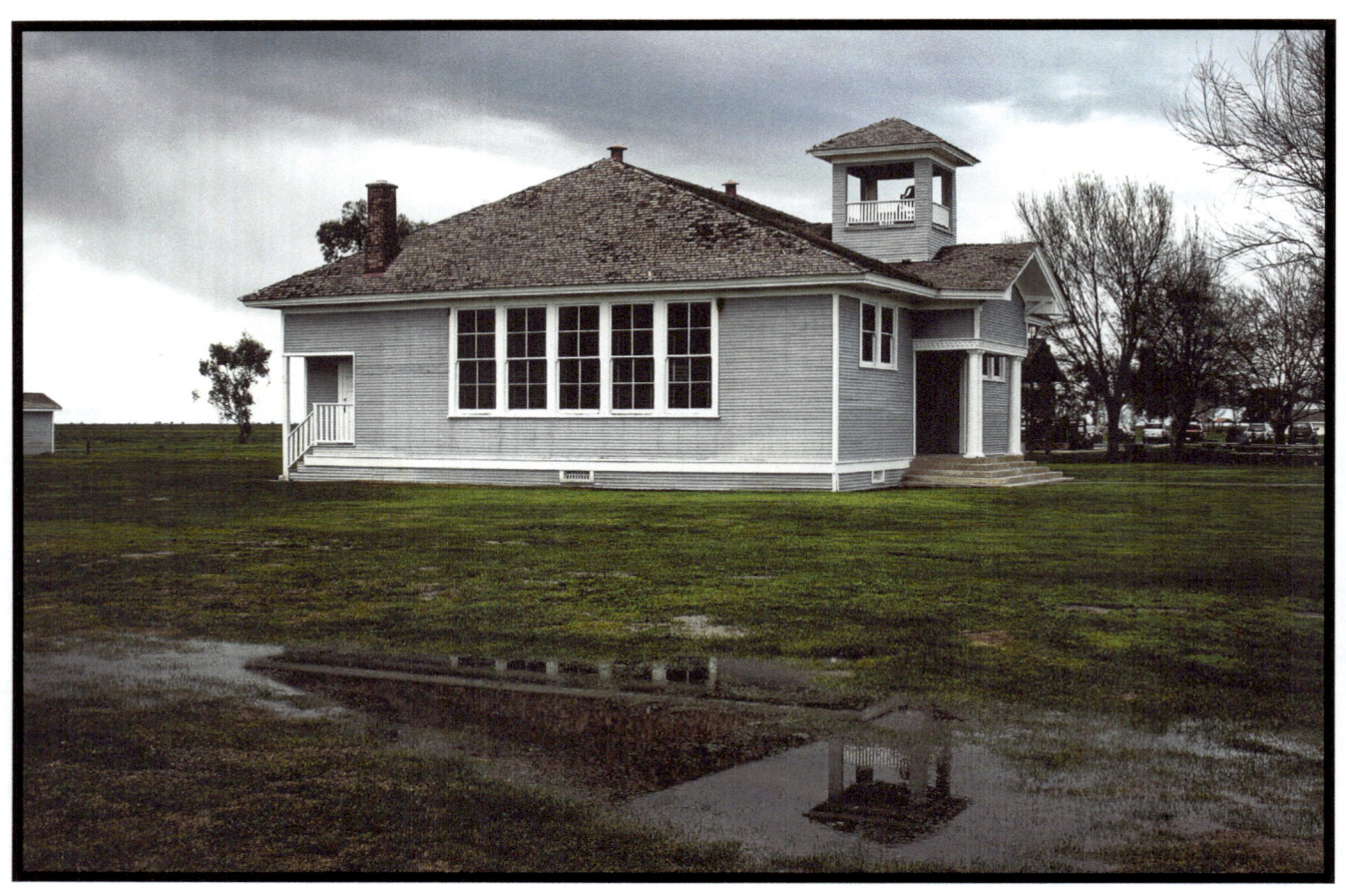

Stormy School Day - Robert Mance

"A side view of Allensworth Elementary Schoolhouse on a rare wet and stormy day."

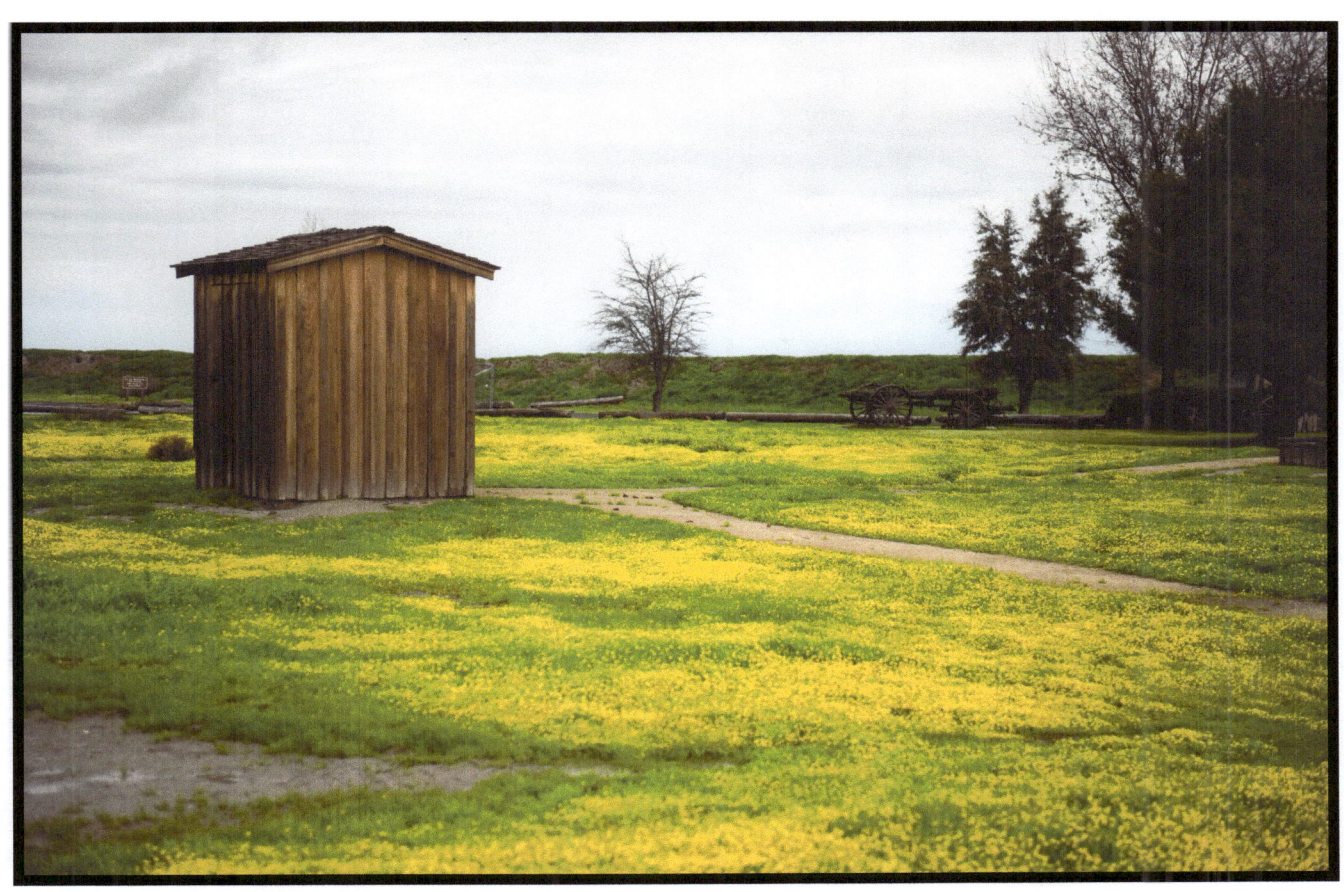

Ground Color - Christy Stallcup

"This beautiful display of color is representative of the Colonel Allensworth State Historic Park. The outbuilding pictured here is located near the park entrance. Notice the old wagon in the background."

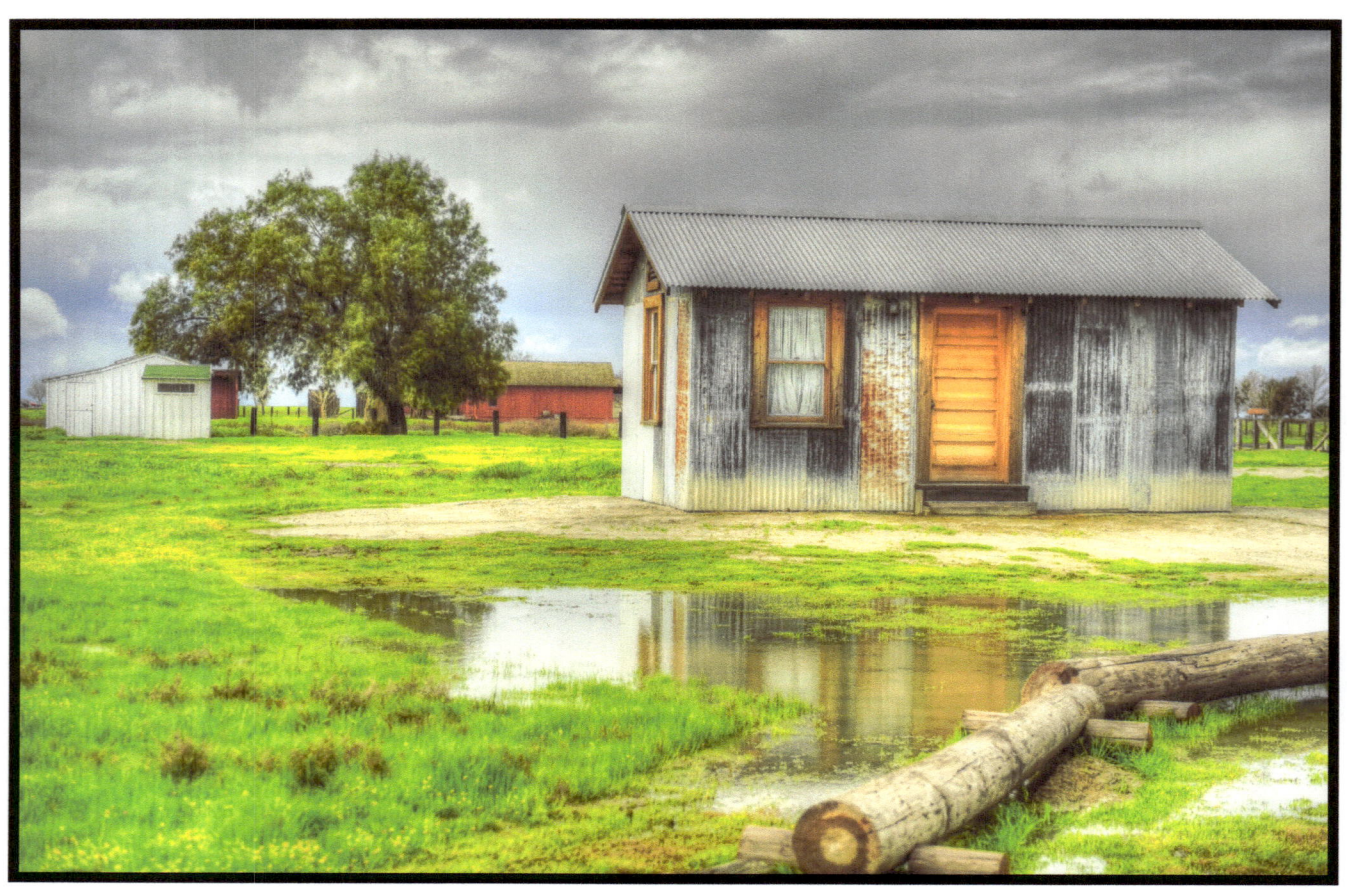

Reflection - Karen Carll

"I loved all of the contrast here. The contrast of the metal and rust against the green of the grass, softened by the reflection. This metal building is also in contrast with the rest of the development of wooden buildings."

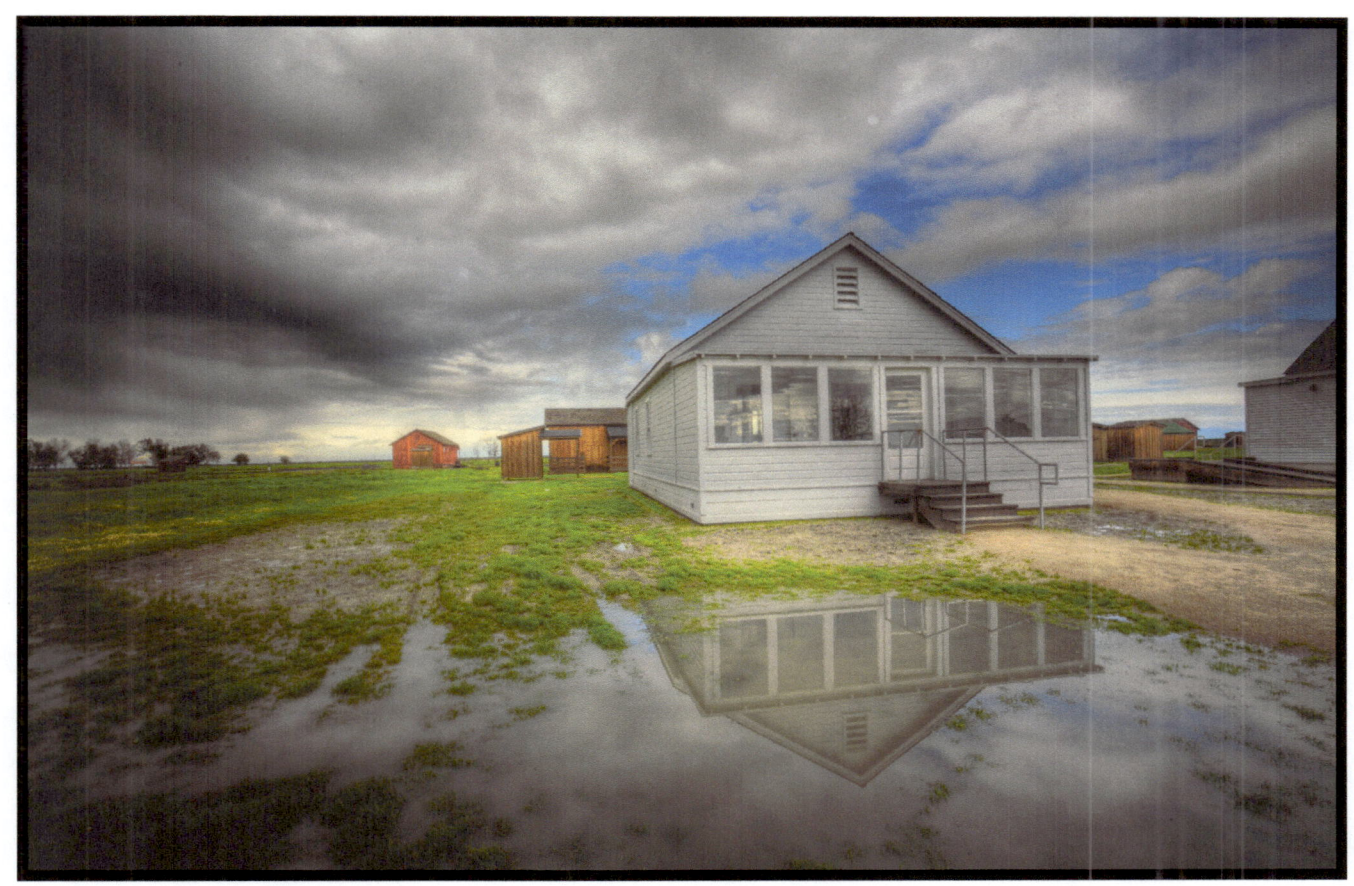

Stormy Reflection - David Paul Green

"This image of the Hackett House is uncharacteristic of Allensworth, which is not typically a stormy place. However, I feel it is representative of the extreme isolation and environmental harshness the settlers faced."

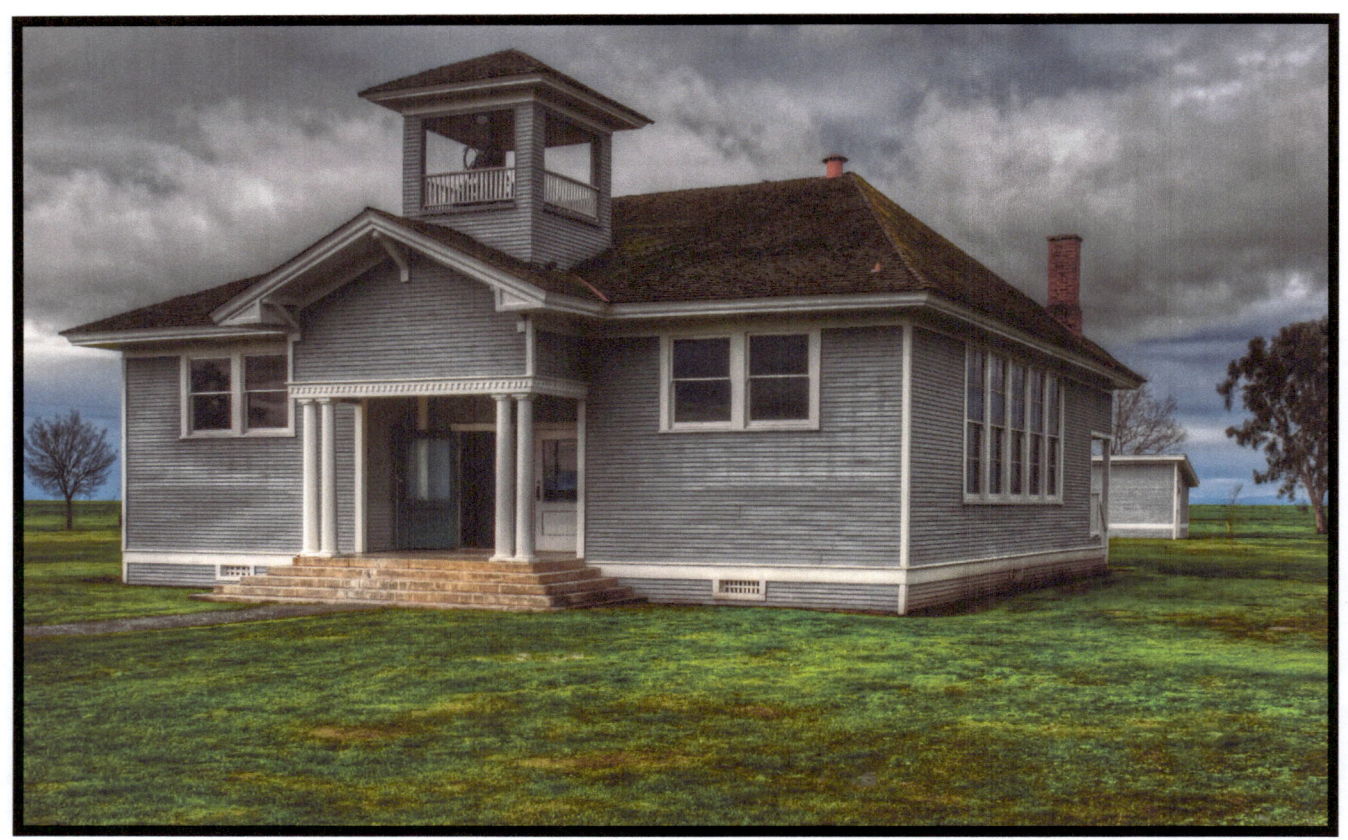

Schoolhouse - Mel Carll

"This building is amazing. Looking at the outside, it looks like an old schoolhouse and you can practically hear the bell ringing. Upon entering the inside, you can sense the learning, complete with teacher's desk, including books and each of the desks where the kids would sit."

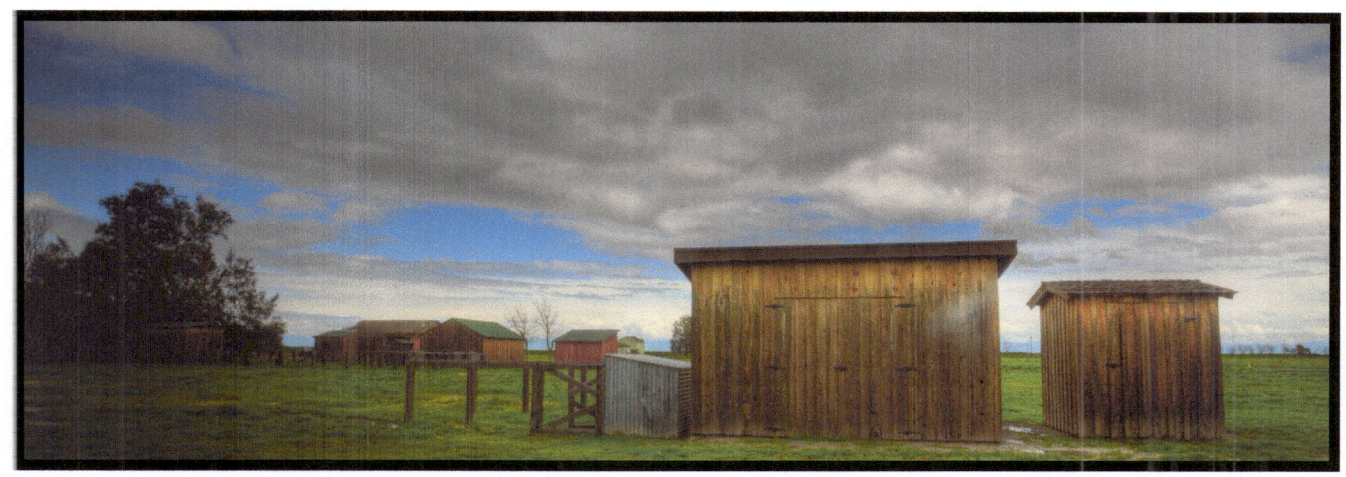

Outbuildings - David Paul Green

"The square symmetry of these buildings is indicative of the sense of order the Allensworth settlers tried to bring to their surroundings. The beauty of the weathered wood only strengthens the functional elegance of these sheds."

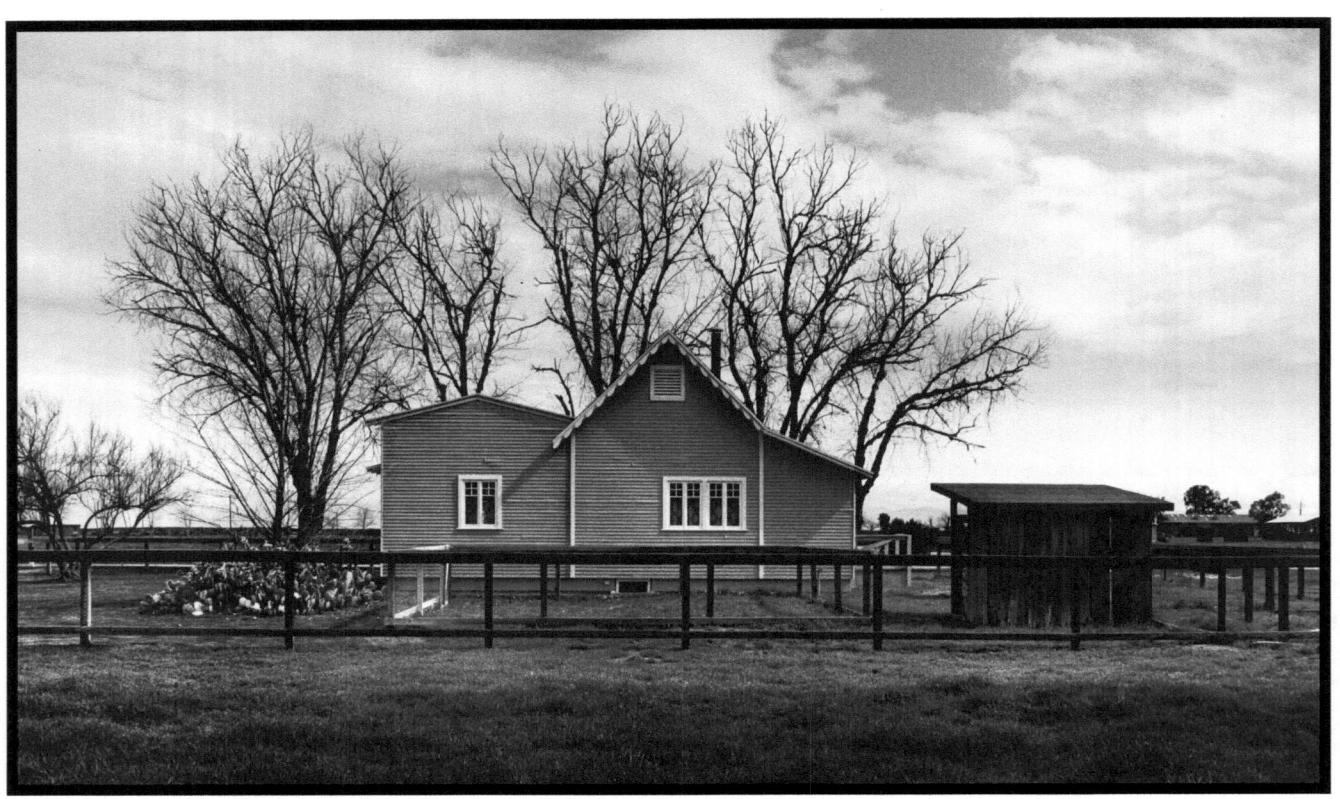

Rear View of Colonel Allensworth's Home - Ted Dayton

"This view, facing east, shows the rear of the Colonel's house on Dunbar Road. His yard is entirely surrounded by fencing. The window on the left is to his bedroom, the other to the kitchen. Visible on the roof above the kitchen window is a vent for the wood-burning stove."

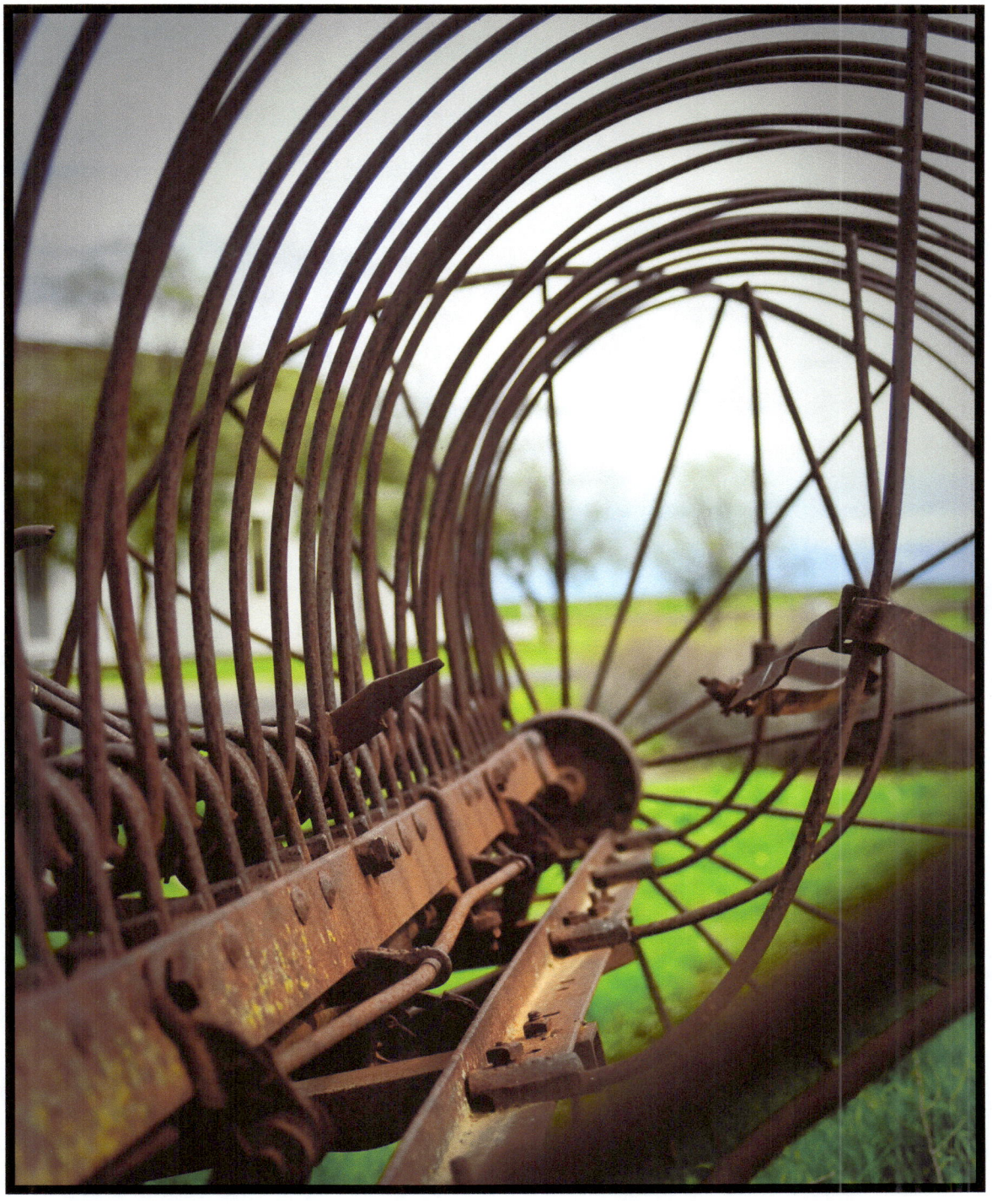

Fallow Hay Rake - Clark Campbell

"This steel wheel hay rake is situated in the vacant lot to the left of the Scott-Gross Store. Hay rakes were used to fluff hay before the hay was stored for winter feeding of livestock."

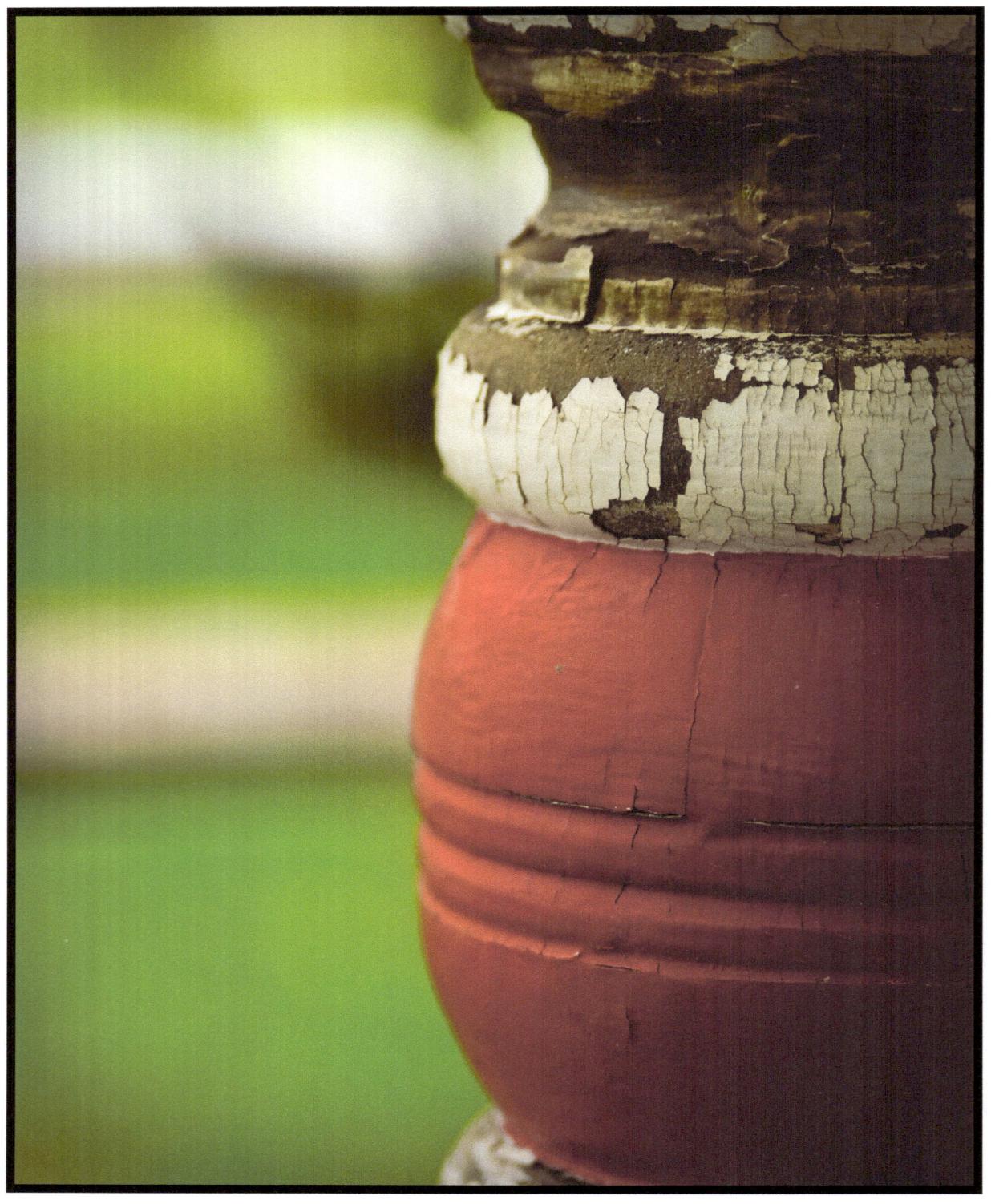

Weatherbeaten Barbershop Pole - Clark Campbell

"Located in front of the reconstruction of Frank Milner's Barbershop. The original barbershop was constructed in 1914 with help from community members."

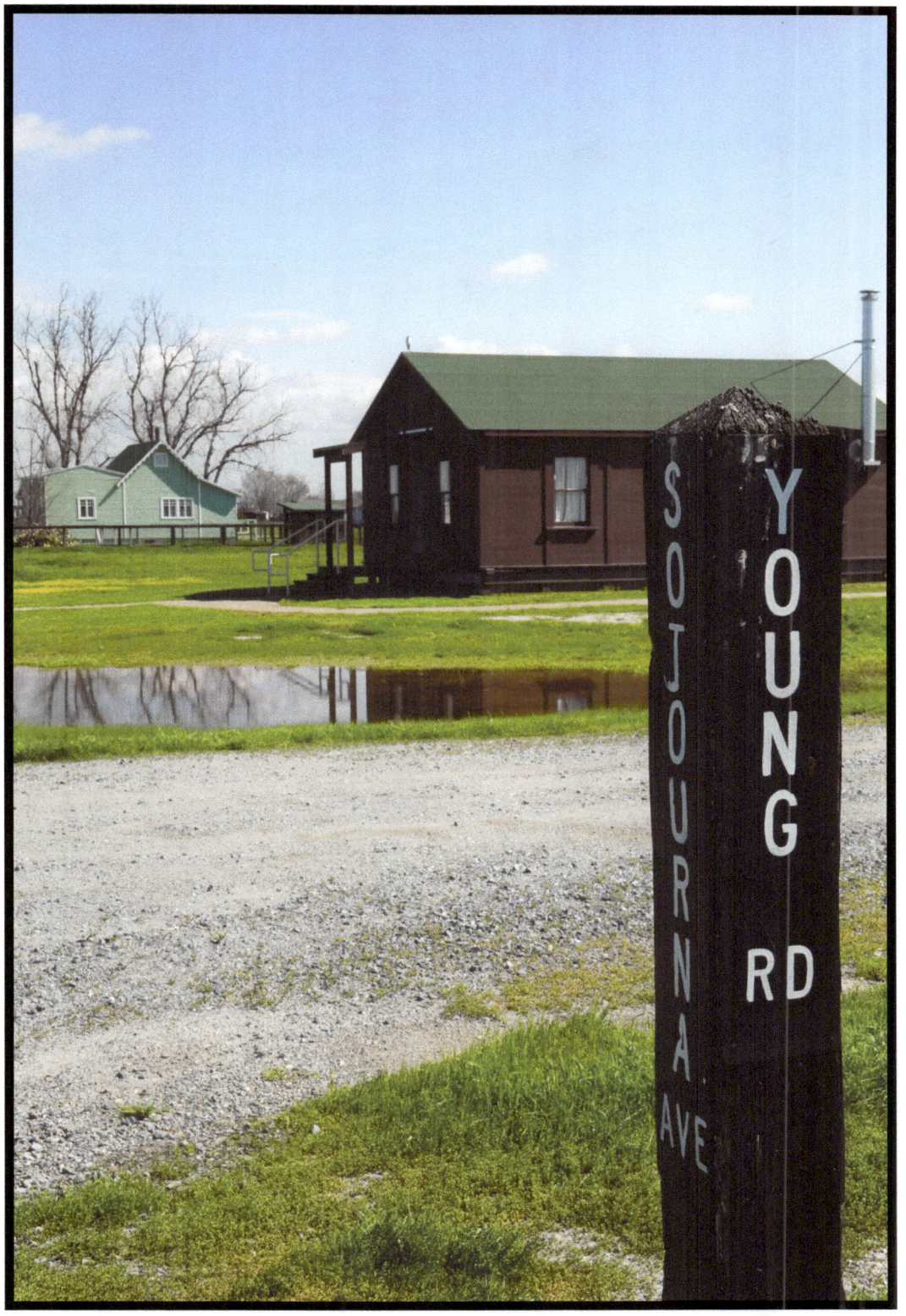

Phillips House - Christy Stallcup

"Colonel Allensworth invited soldiers from his regiment to live in Allensworth. Sergeant James Phillips and his wife, Birdie, raised their four children in this home."

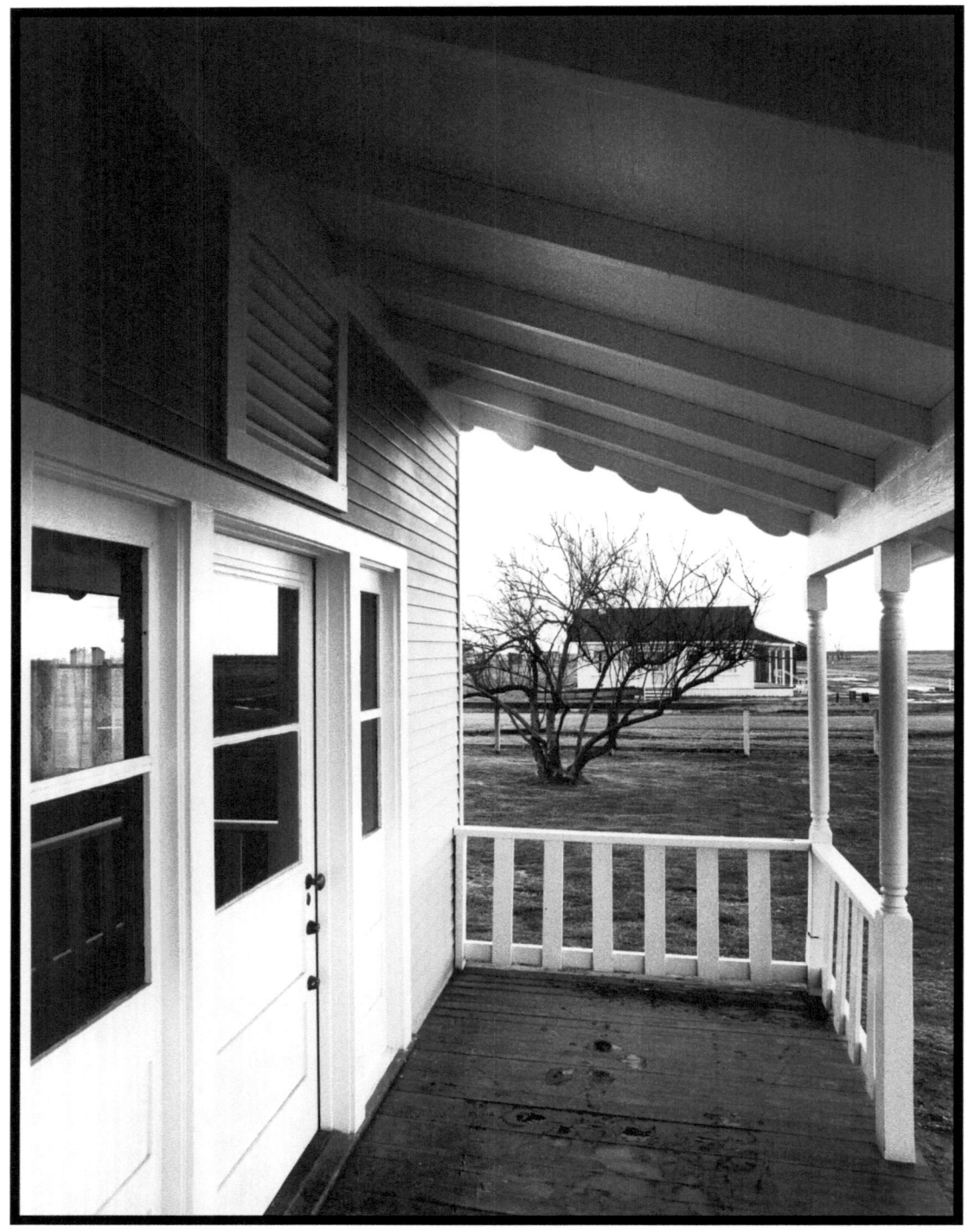

Front Porch of Colonel Allensworth's Home - Ted Dayton (cover image)

"Colonel Allensworth's home on Dunbar Road faces east, toward the railroad tracks only a few hundreds yards away. It is easy to imagine seeing and hearing the trains passing by while sitting on his covered porch or from the shade of large trees in the front yard. The front door to the Colonel's home is rather short; a man just barely over six feet tall might have to stoop to pass through."

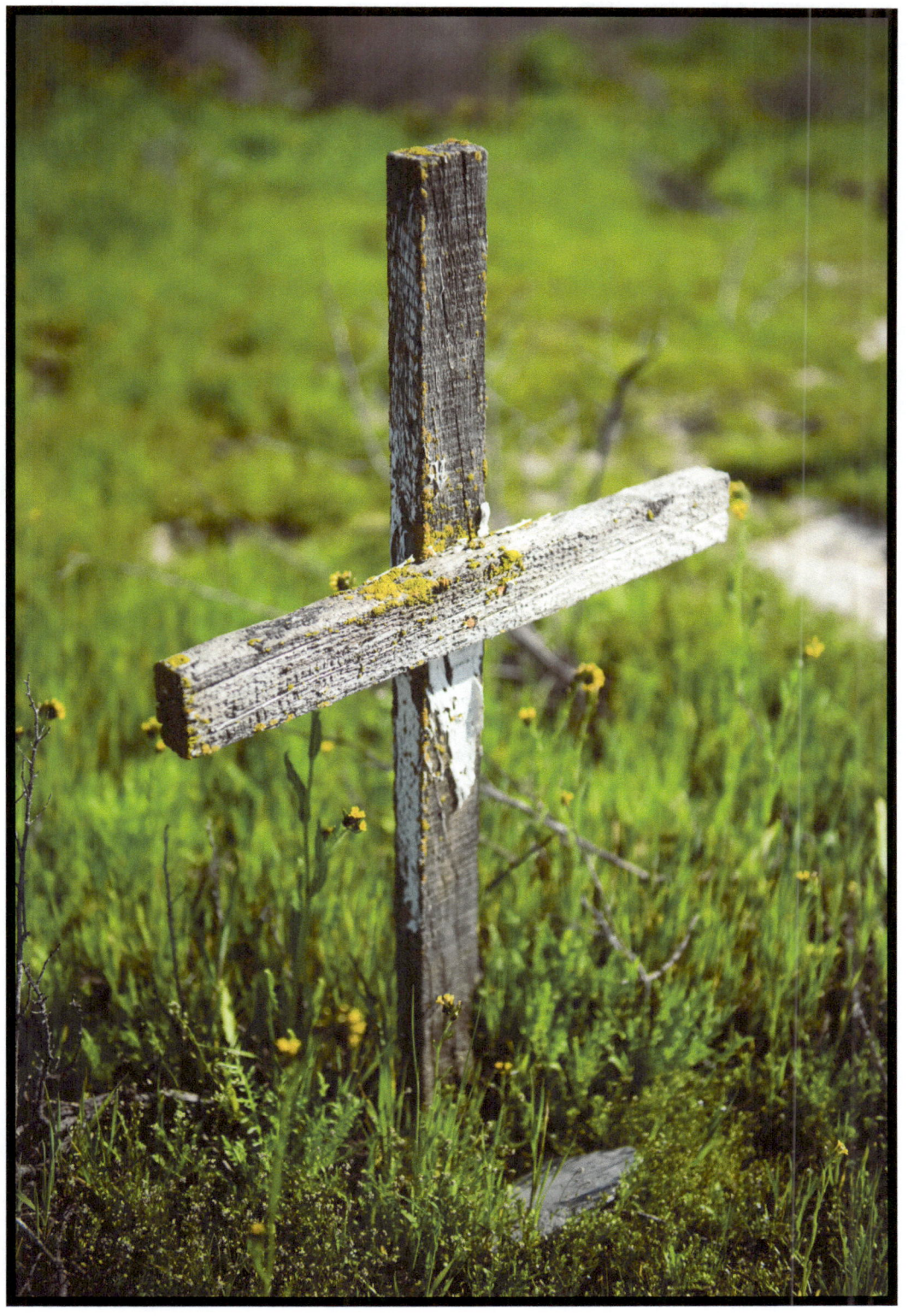

Grave Marker – Allensworth Cemetery - Christy Stallcup

"The first cemetery in Allensworth was established in 1911. It is now considered a historical site on the edge of town."

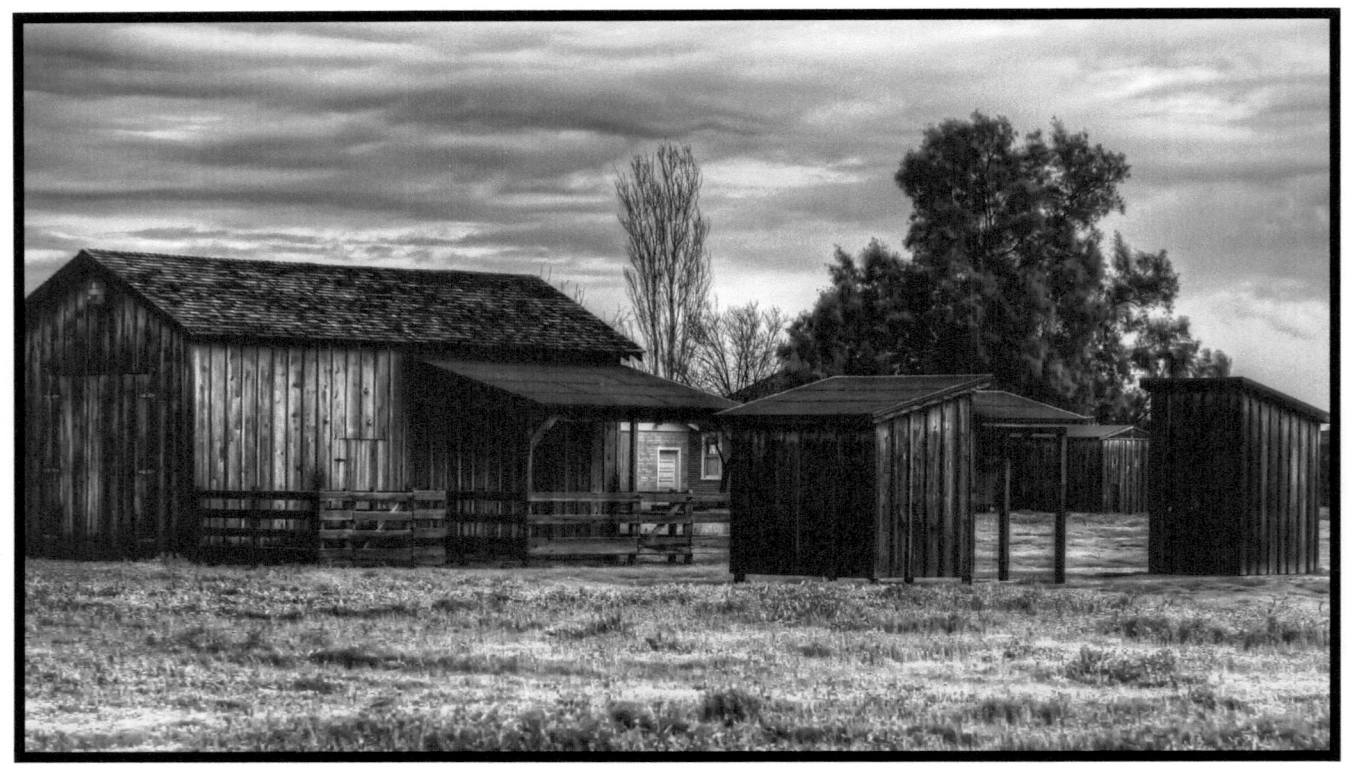

Noble Barn on a Stormy Day - Mel Carll

"As I looked out at this barn, you could sense how the storms, sun and years have aged these old buildings, yet they stand so proud. These were the type of buildings scattered throughout the area."

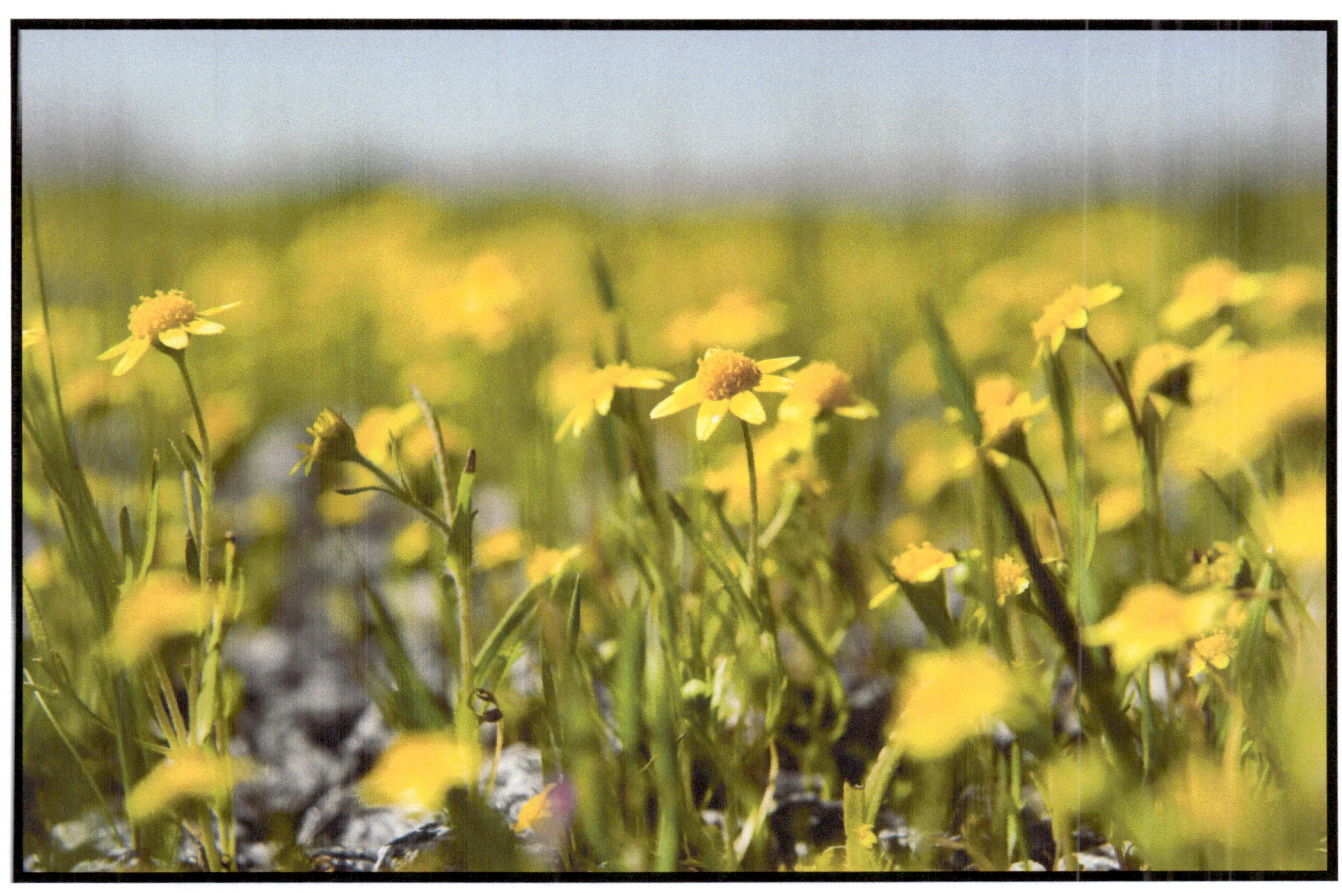

Full Bloom - Christy Stallcup

"Wildflowers are commonplace in the springtime in Allensworth."

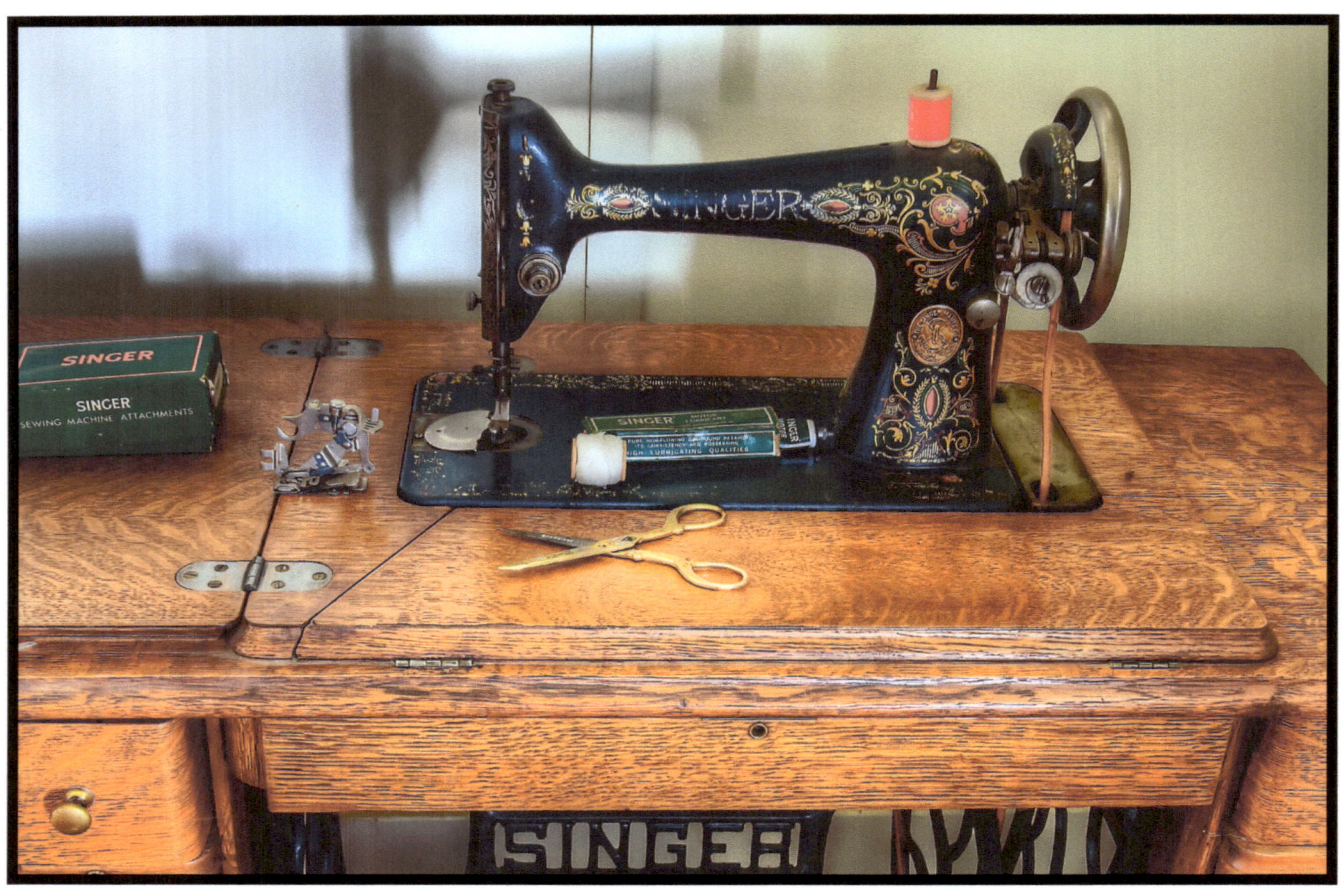

Old Singer - Mel Carll

"This machine has seen lots of use. You can imagine all the clothes that have been made using this old Singer. It makes me think of all the clothes my mom made when I was a kid, on her Singer sewing machine."

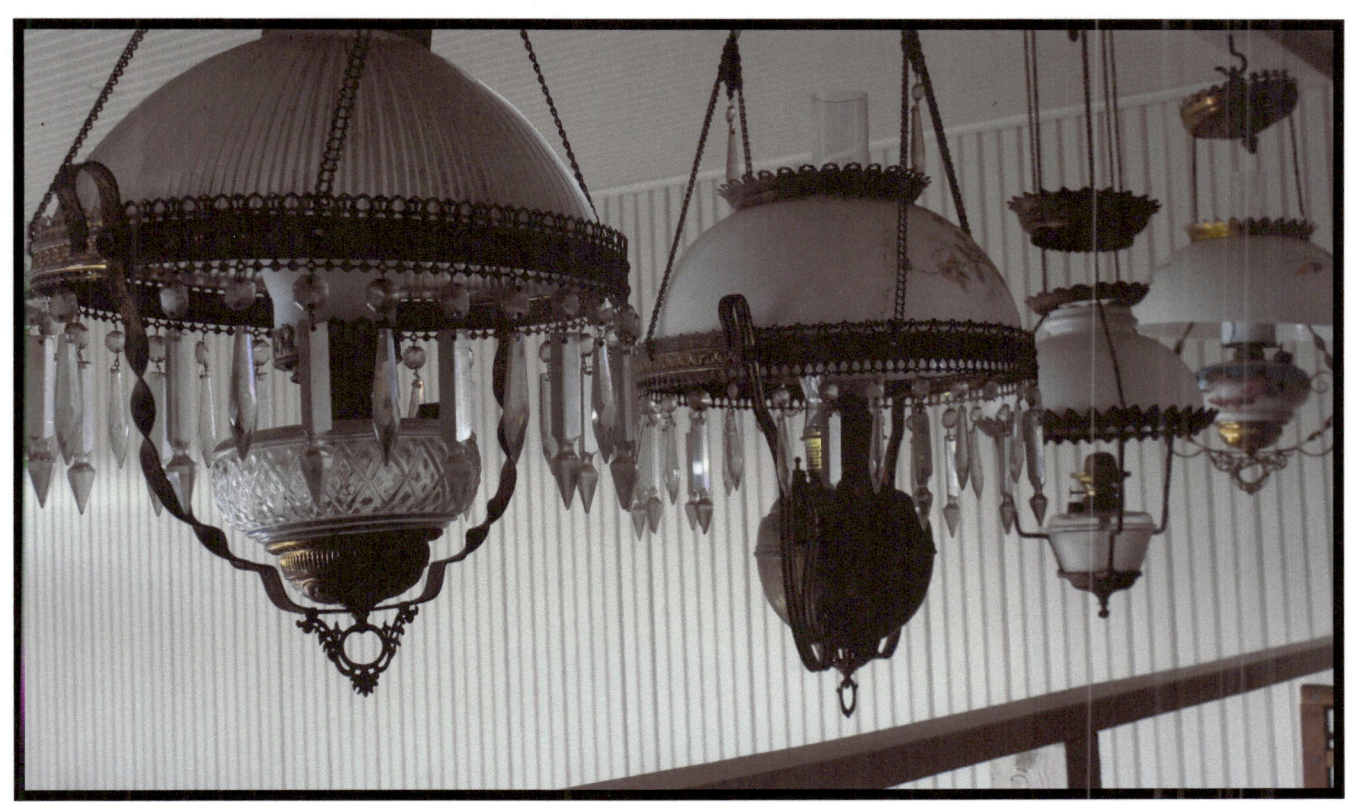

Fine Lighting - April Bielefeldt

"Lights for sale in the Hindsman Store. The store was built in 1911 and became the the longest-lasting business in Allensworth, serving the community for 35 years. The store is a wonderful place and sold a variety of goods from candy to seeds to tools."

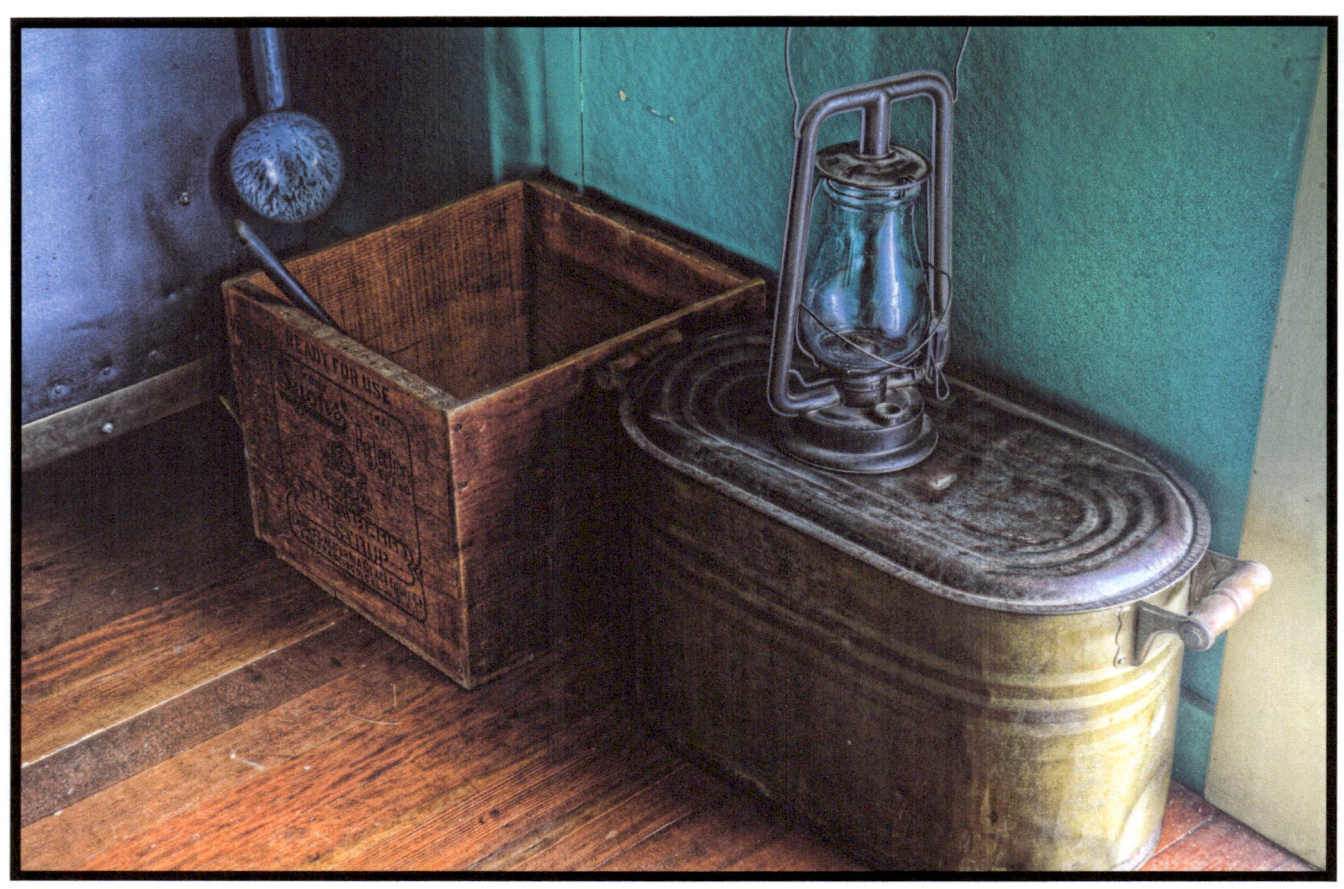

Kitchen Objects - David Paul Green

"The intensity of the juxtaposed textures, shapes and colors compelled me to take this high dynamic range (HDR) image of the Smith House kitchen. In such a practical living space, function becomes beauty."

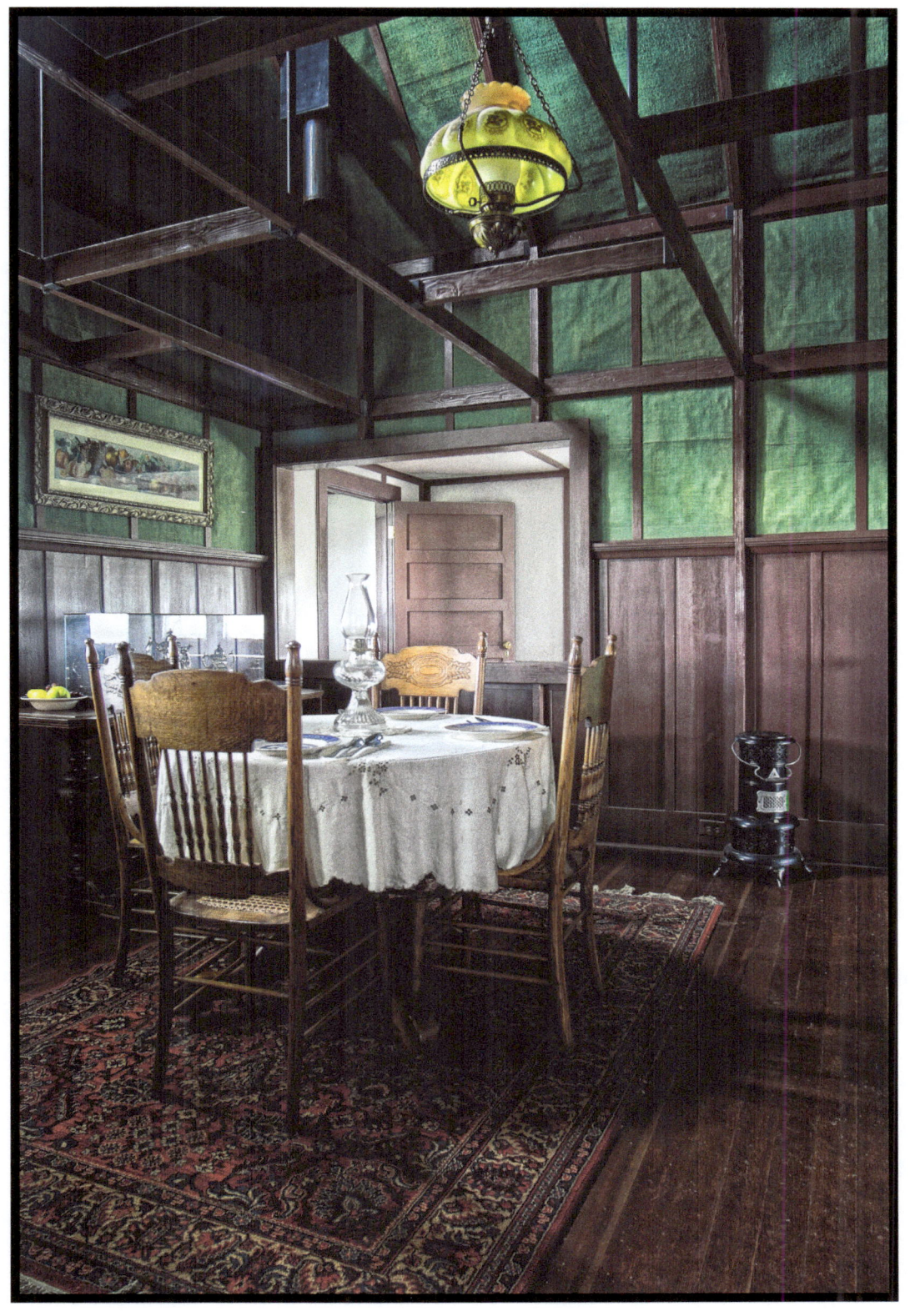

Supper Time at the Colonel Allensworth House - Robert Mance

"The dining room at Colonel Allensworth house, beautifully set with his best china."

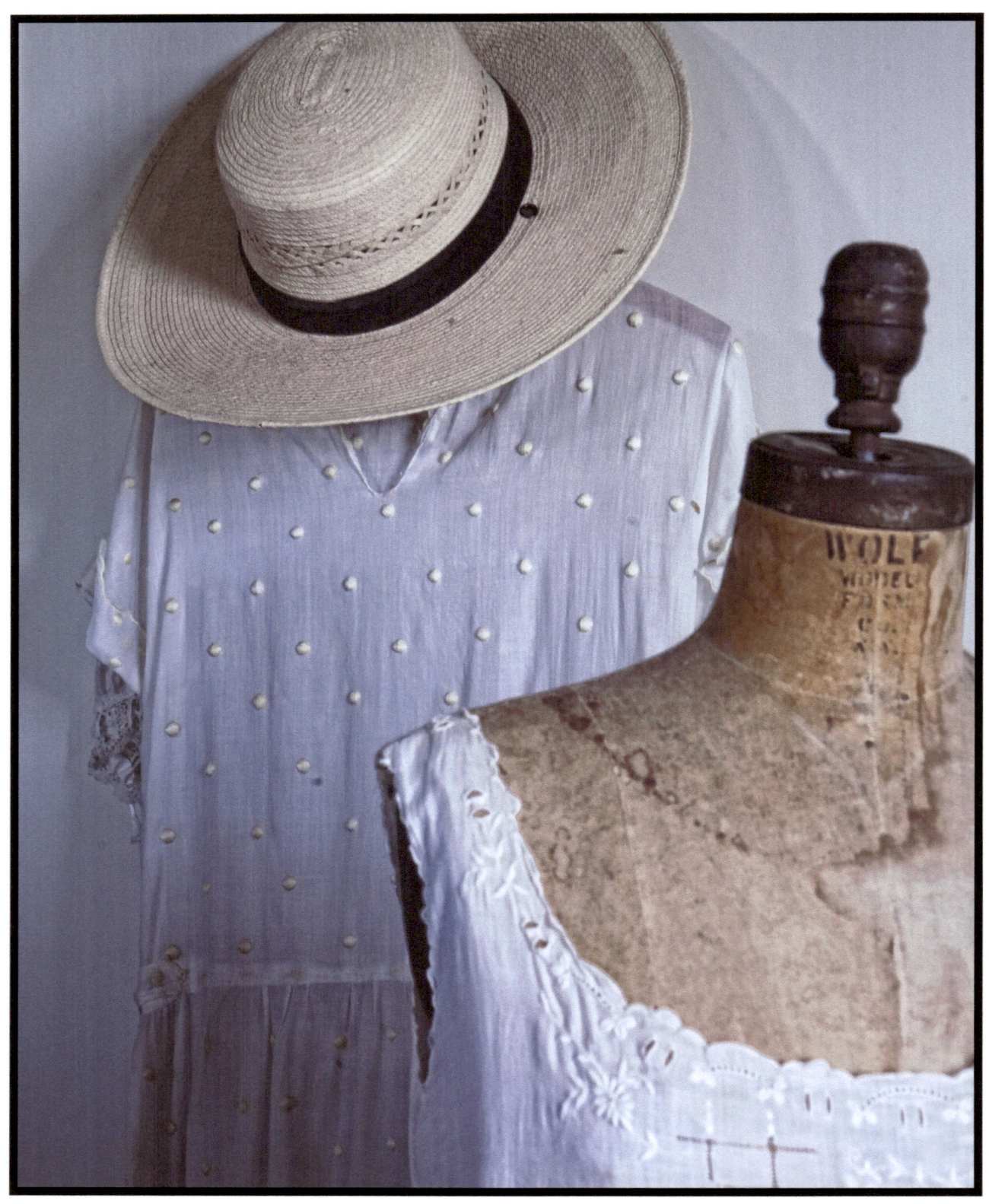

Sunday Best- Frank Smith House - Jean Carter

"Located in the bedroom of the Frank Smith House. These clothing items bring to mind, that the ladies took great care in laying out their clothes. Perhaps this was Mrs. Smith's Sunday best."

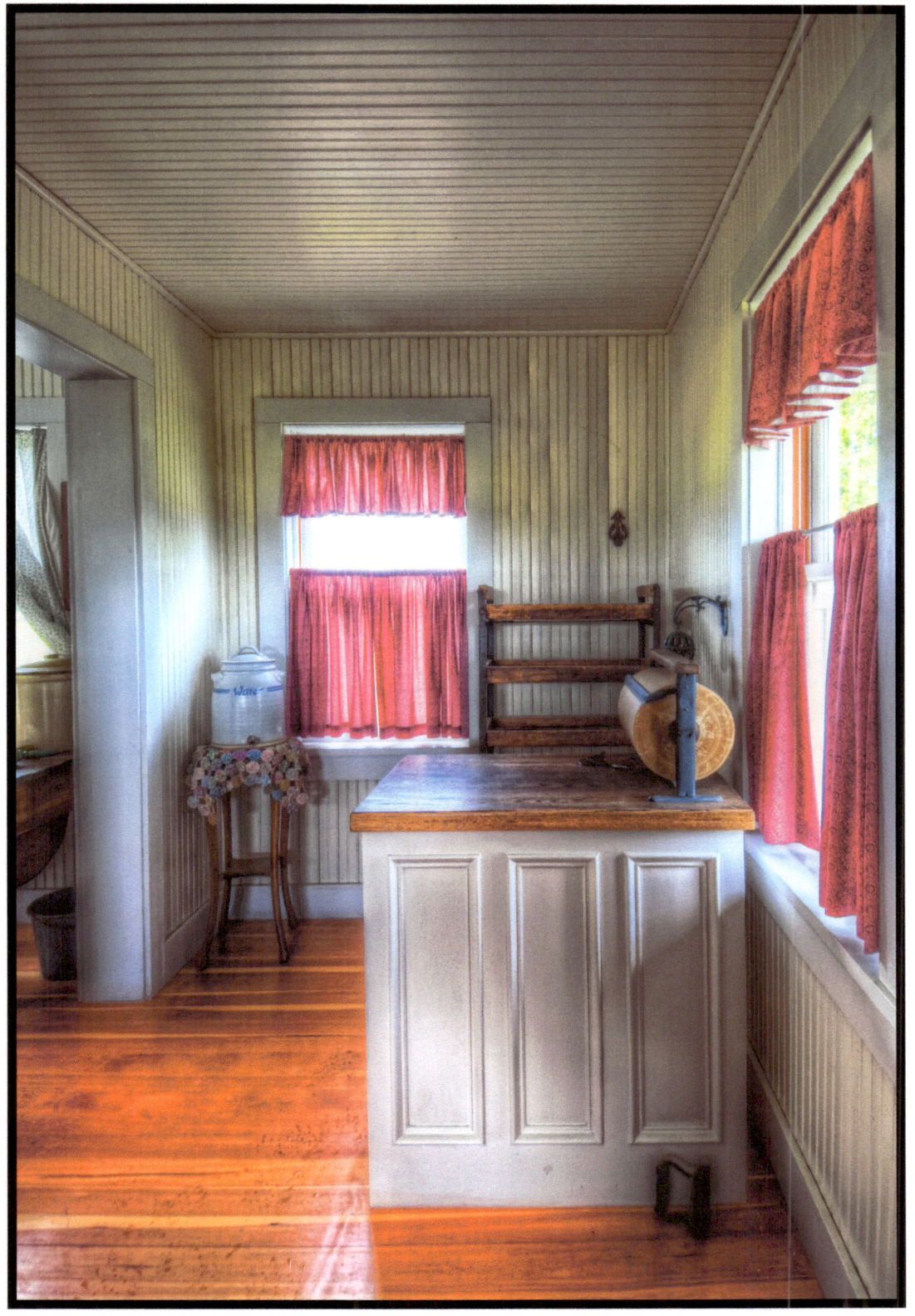

Kitchen Counter - Mel Carll

"I loved how bright this room was. You can picture the meals and baking taking place."

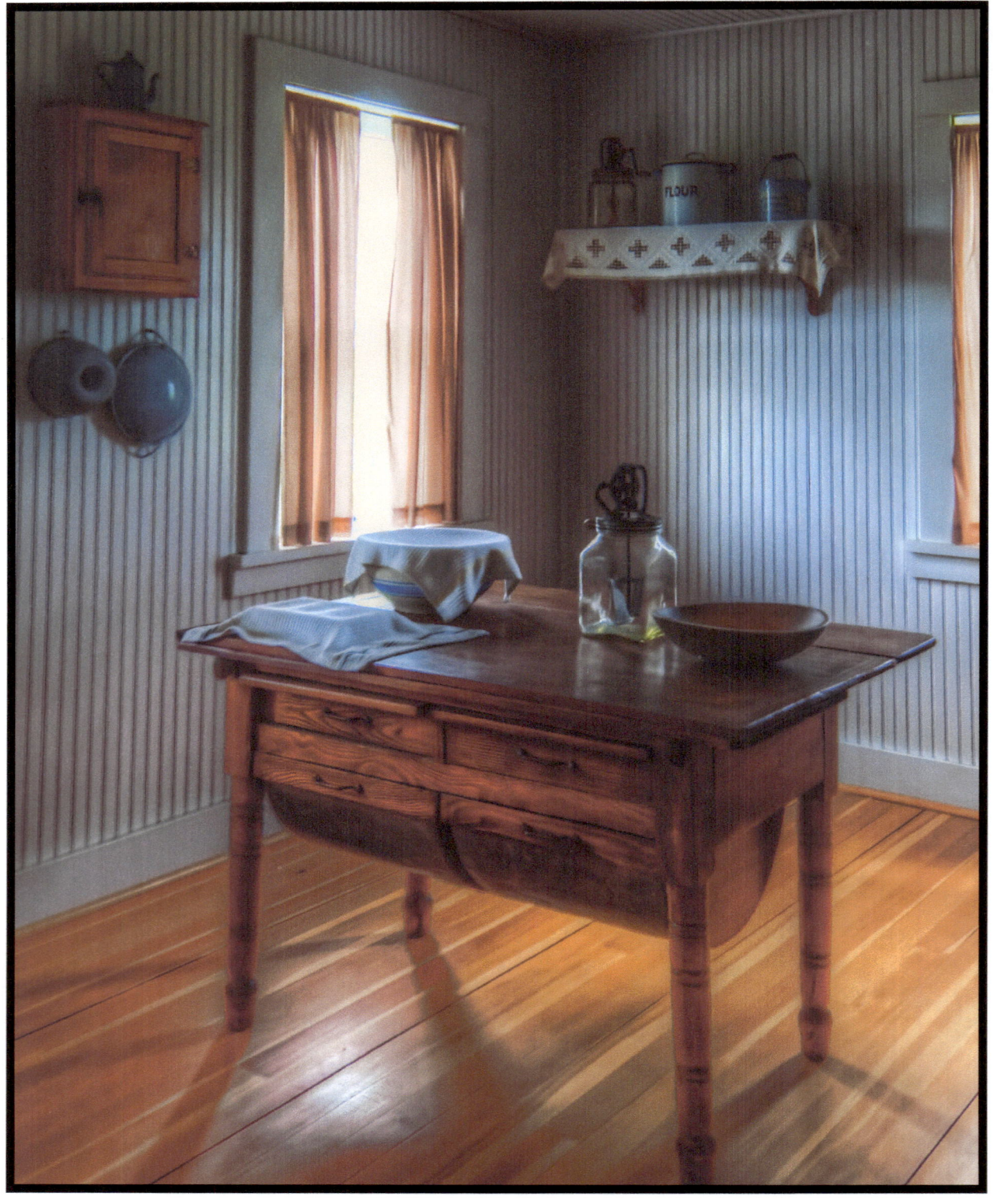

Prep Table - Mel Carll

"Looking at this table, I could smell the pie baking as I snapped the photograph."

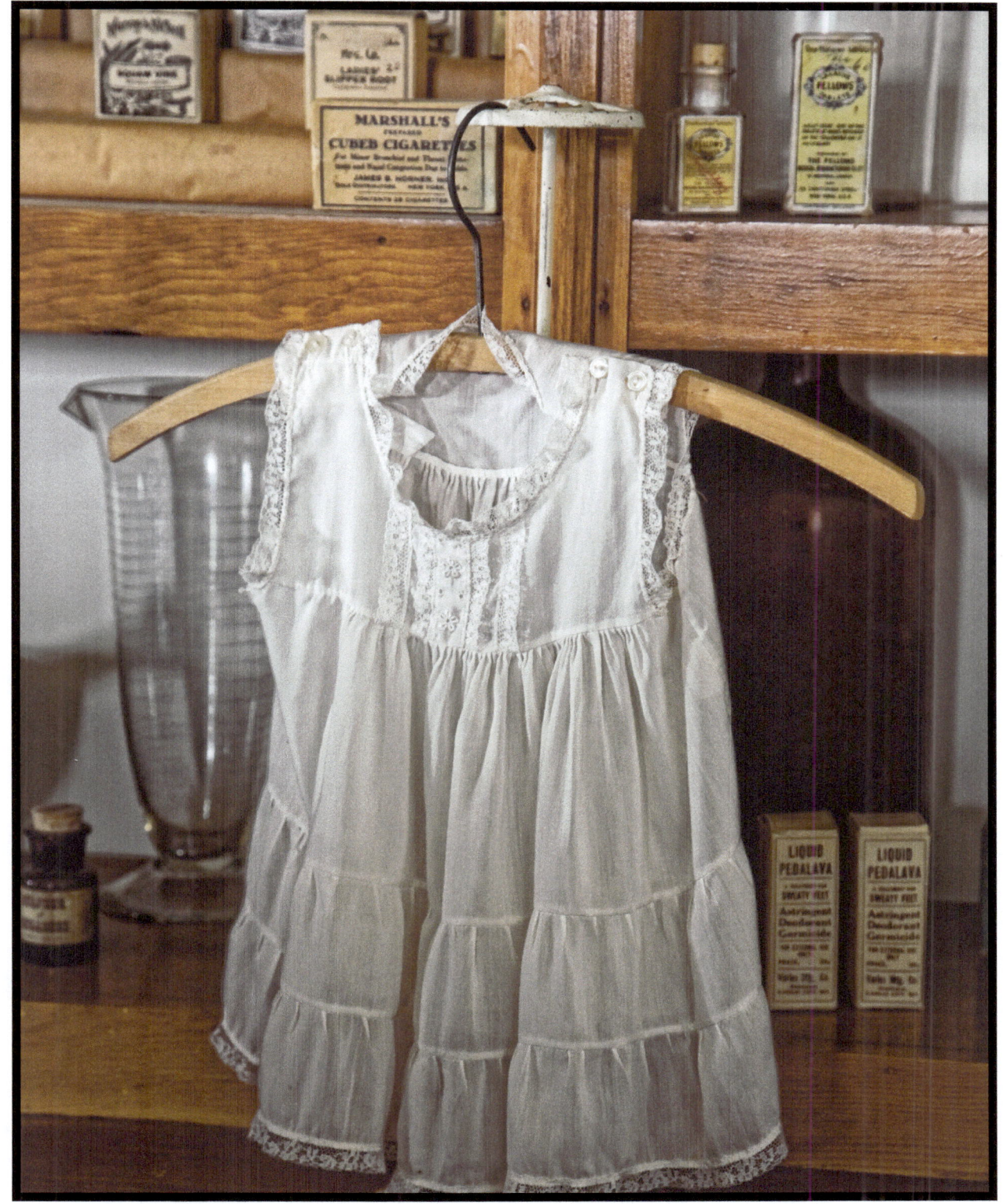

Girl's Undergament - Jean Carter

"Located in the Allensworth Cash Store aka Singleton General Store & Post Office, which was operated by Joshua Singleton. This item represents that store's wide array of products providing everything the residence would need from clothing to kerosene lamps to perishables."

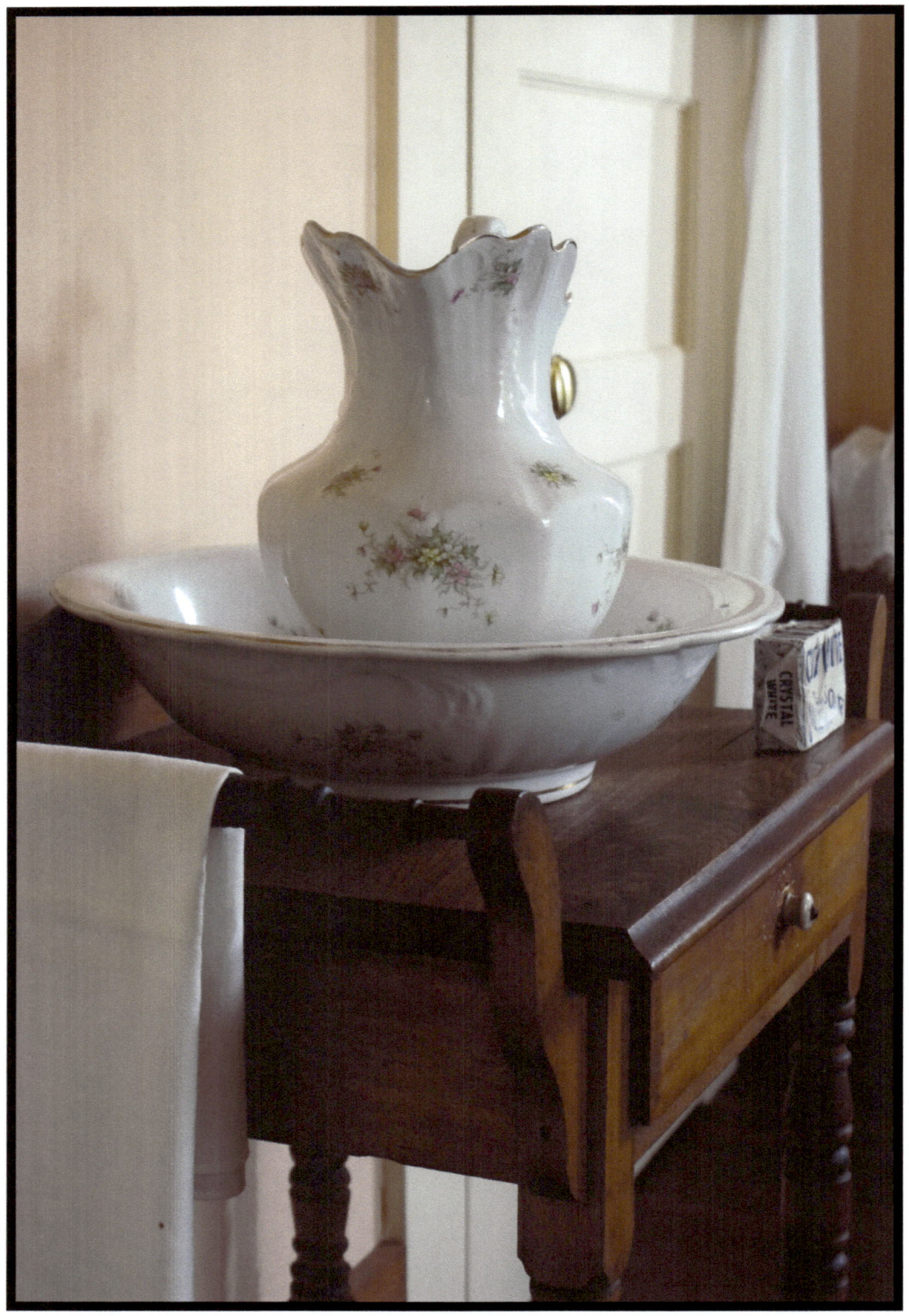

Simple - April Bielefeldt

"This is a porcelain pitcher and wash bowl. With most homes having no plumbing, each bedroom would have a wash bowl and pitcher. This is from one of the Smith House bedrooms. The home, which had three bedrooms, was built in 1910. The following year, Mrs. Smith was widowed and needed to rent the extra rooms for boarders."

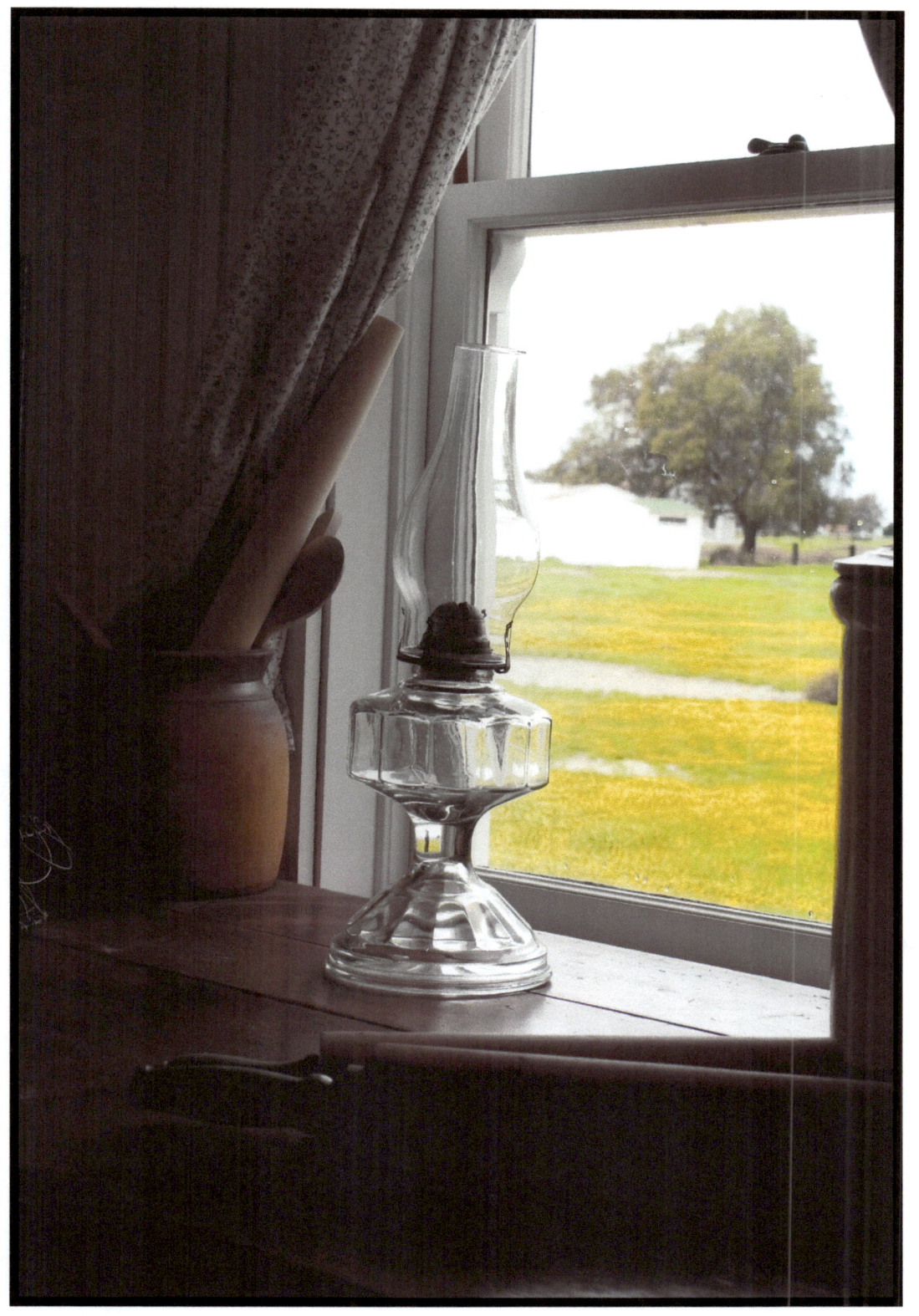

Kitchen Window - April Bielefeldt

"This is looking through the kitchen window of the Dotson house, which was built around 1914 when they opened a restaurant in the front of the house. The Dotsons continued the restaurant until about 1919, when they moved to Fresno."

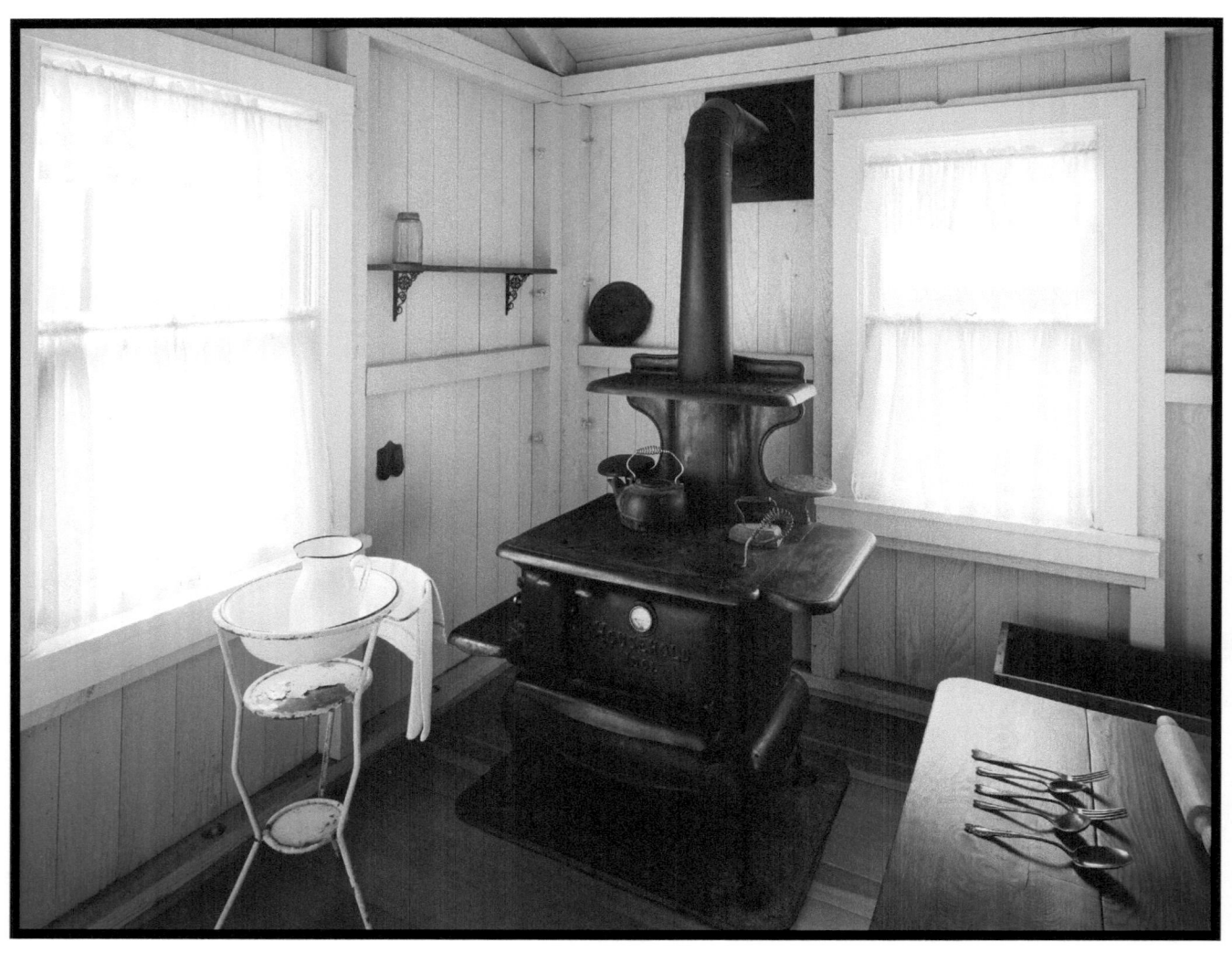

Stove in Phillips House Kitchen - Rick Russell

"The kitchen of the Phillips family house."

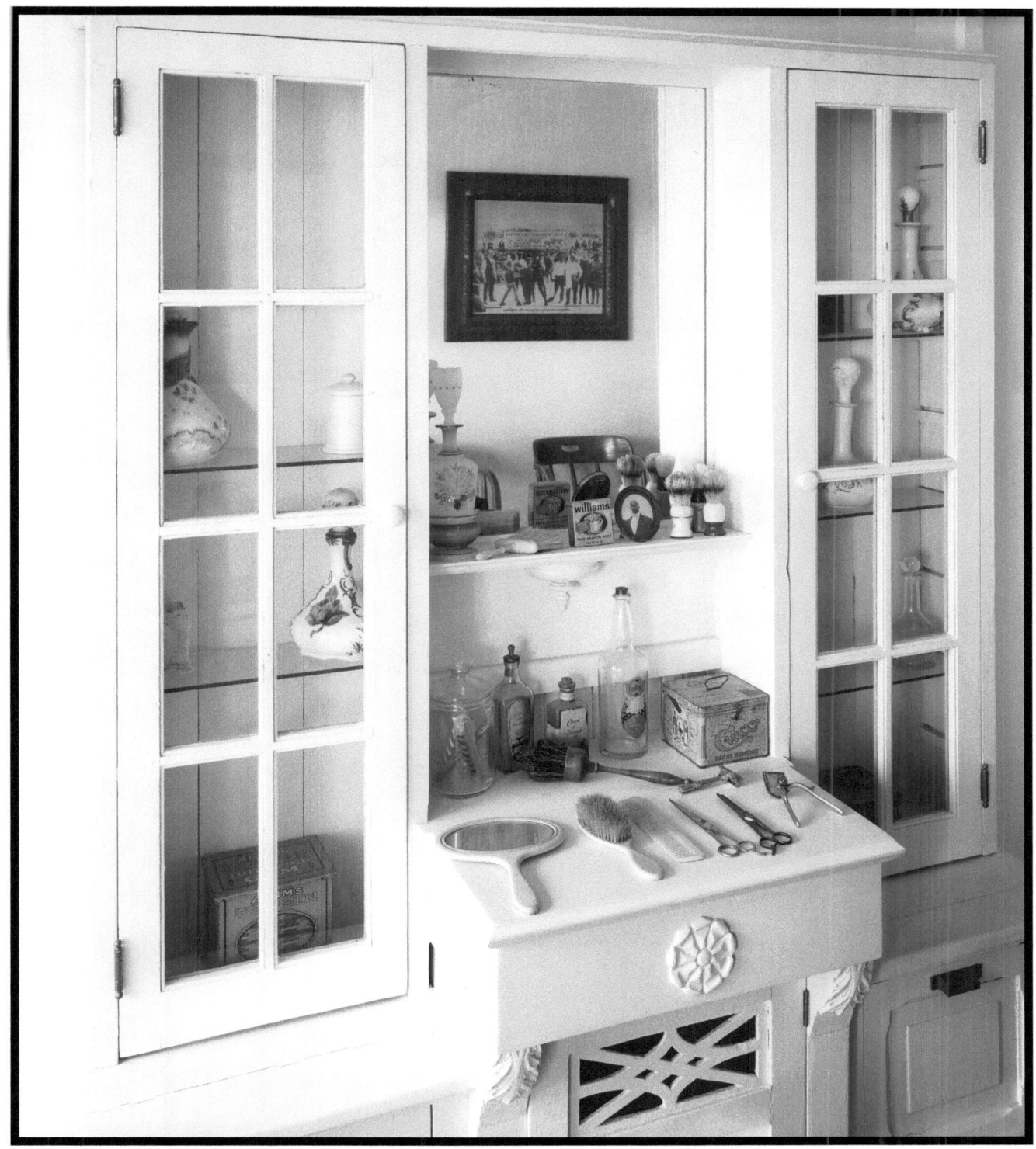

Shelving in Milner House and Barbershop - Rick Russell

"The shelves and mirror in the Milner House and Barbershop. Note that the large photograph in the center of the shelves is a reflection of a photo located on the opposite wall."

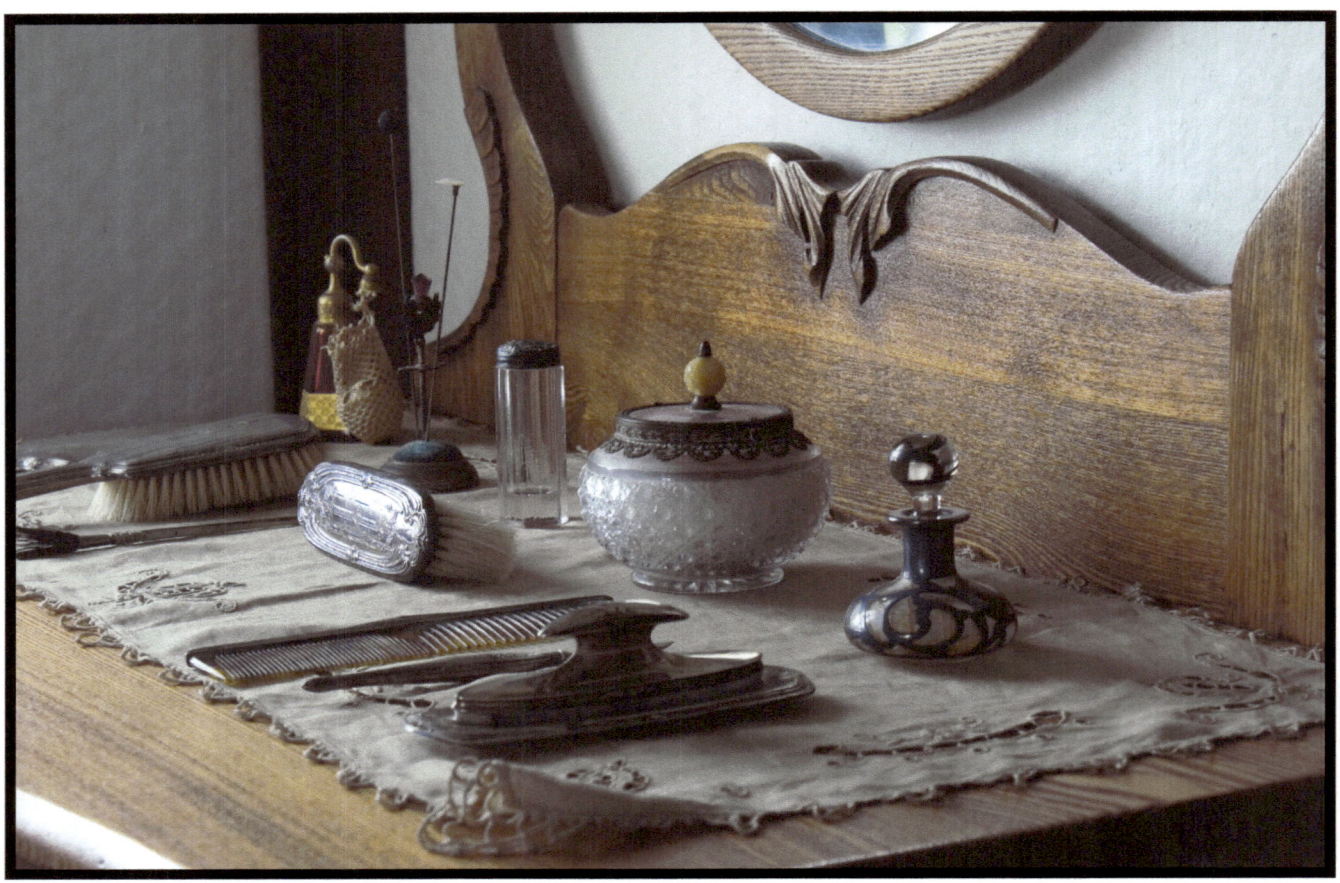

A Lady's Dresser - April Bielefeldt

"Allen Allensworth was the founder of the town and this was his dream. His home here was assembled in 1911. This was a prefabricated home delivered by rail. The Allensworth family split their time between their Los Angeles home and this home in Allensworth. The dresser is a fine example of the dreams this man had for this unique community."

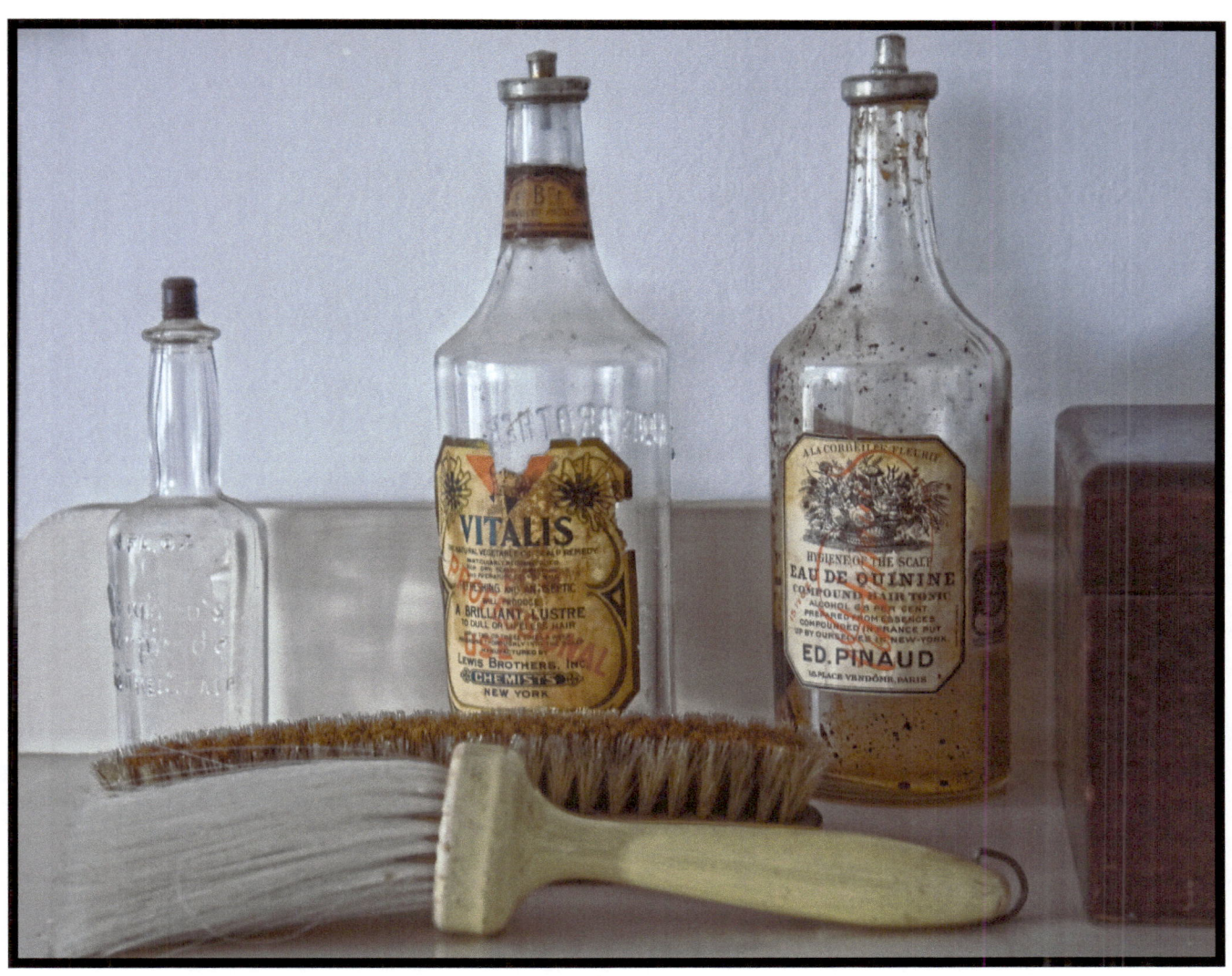

The Barbershop - Jean Carter

"Frank Milner's barbershop served as an informal men's social center. These bottles represent the latest products to assist the male population of Allensworth to look their finest."

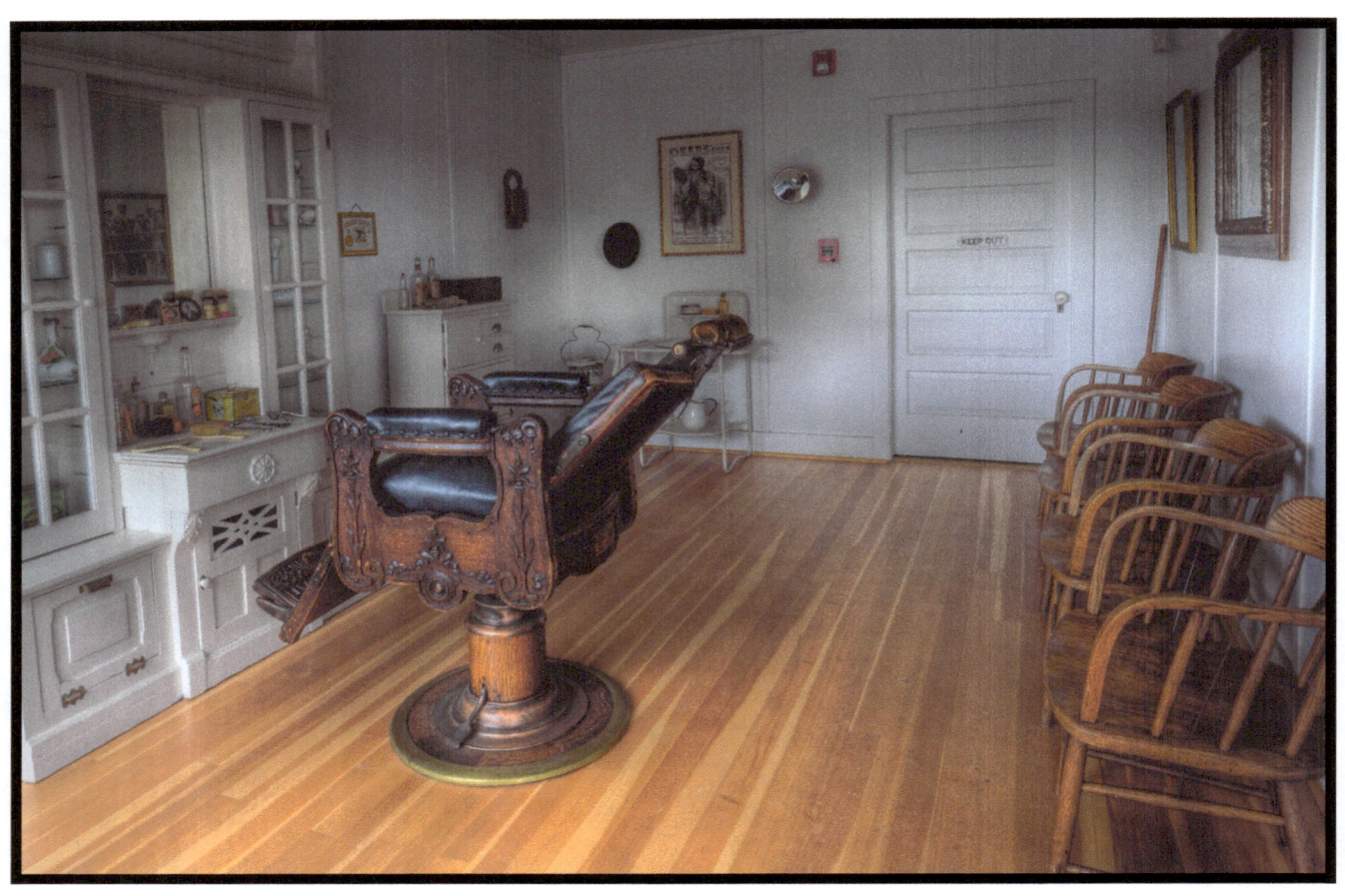

Barbershop - David Paul Green

"Thinking of my contemporary barbershop experiences, I wonder whether Frank Milner's barbershop was a raucous place of male camaraderie, or a serious place of support and reflection in a town where the challenges were so daunting. Either way, the conversations must have been stimulating!"

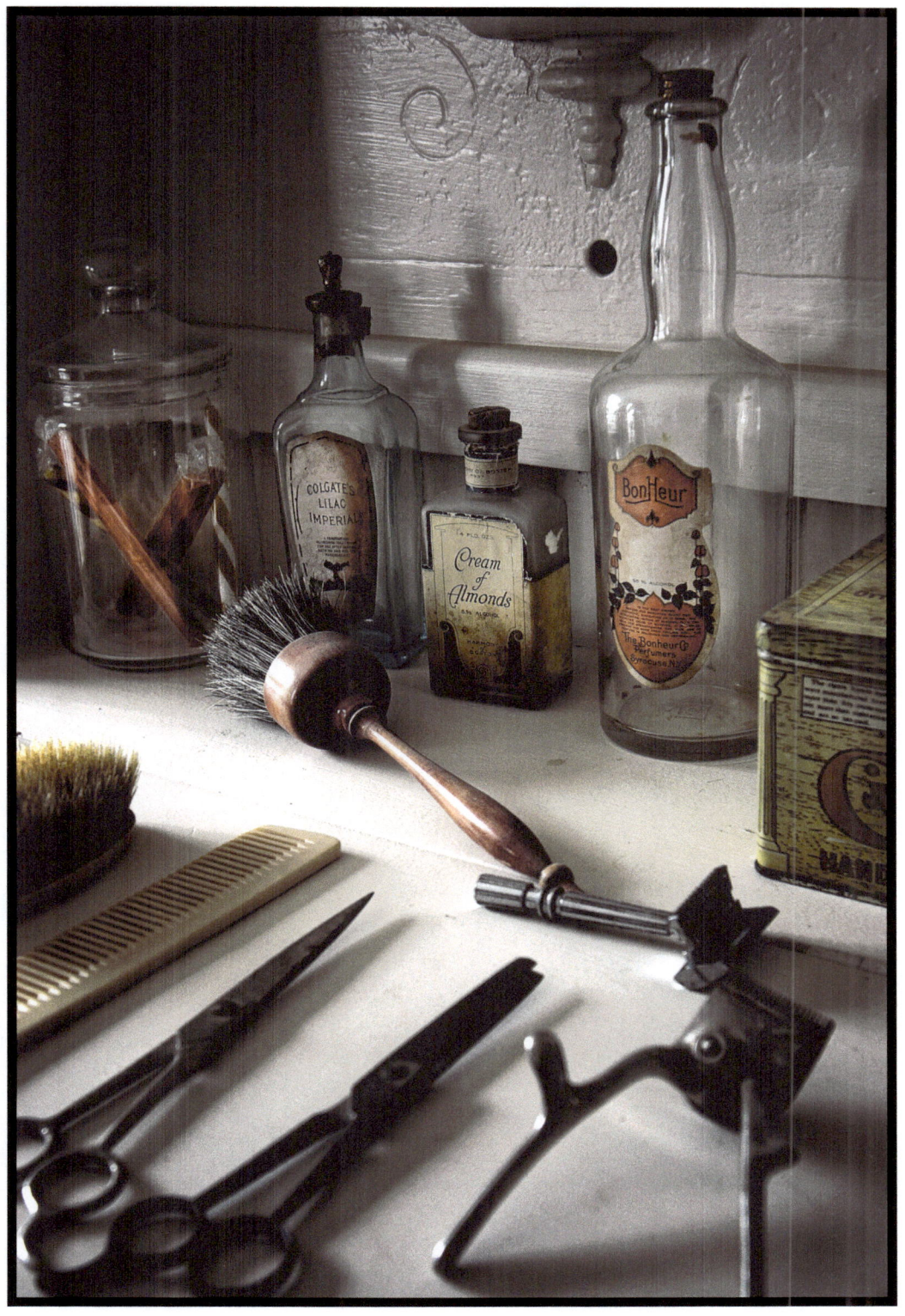

Barbershop Tools - Robert Mance

"Tools of the trade at the Milner House and Barbershop, helping keep the men of Allensworth looking their very best."

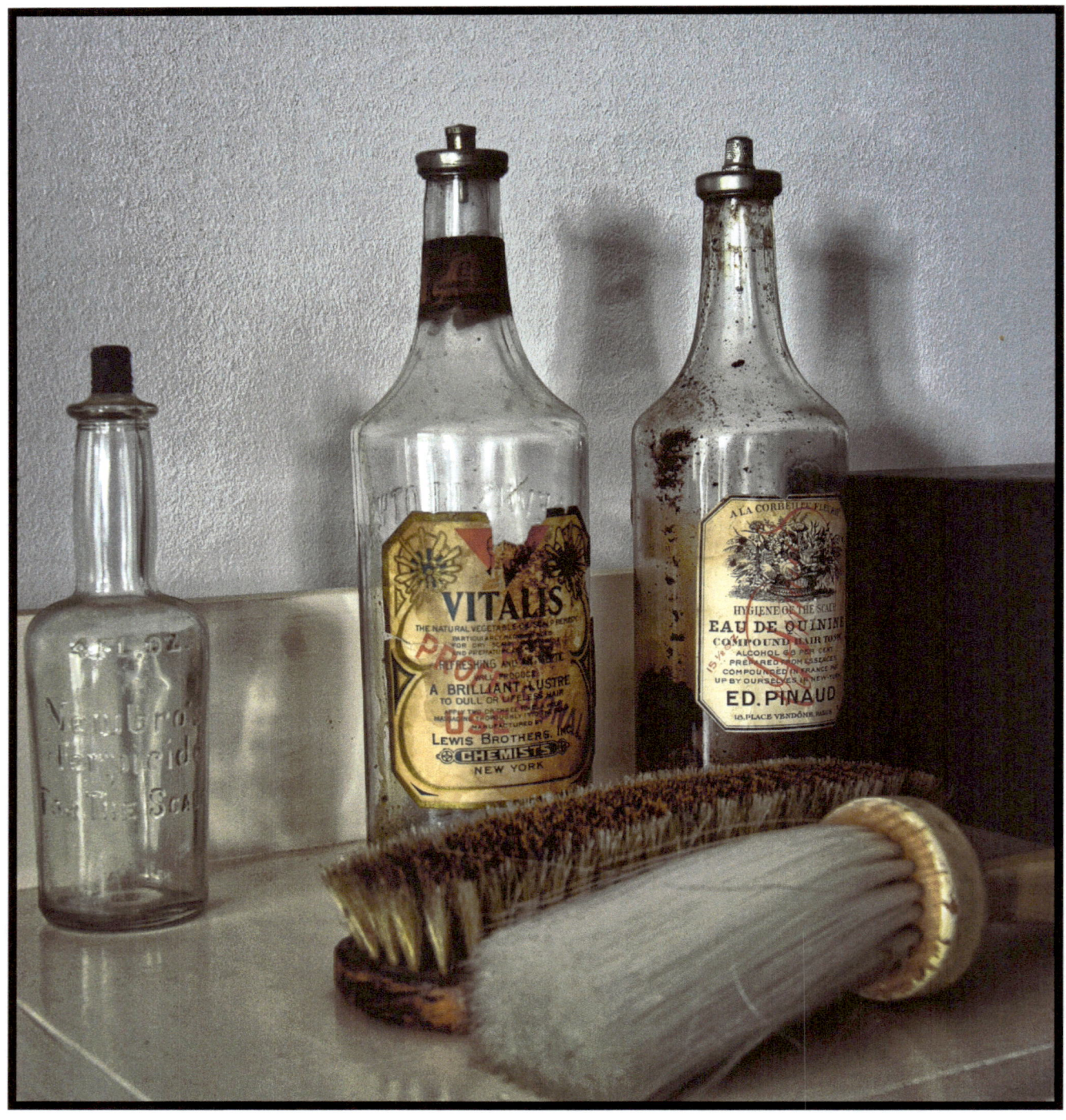

Barbershop Bottles - Robert Mance

"For that final touchup after a haircut at the Milner House and Barbershop."

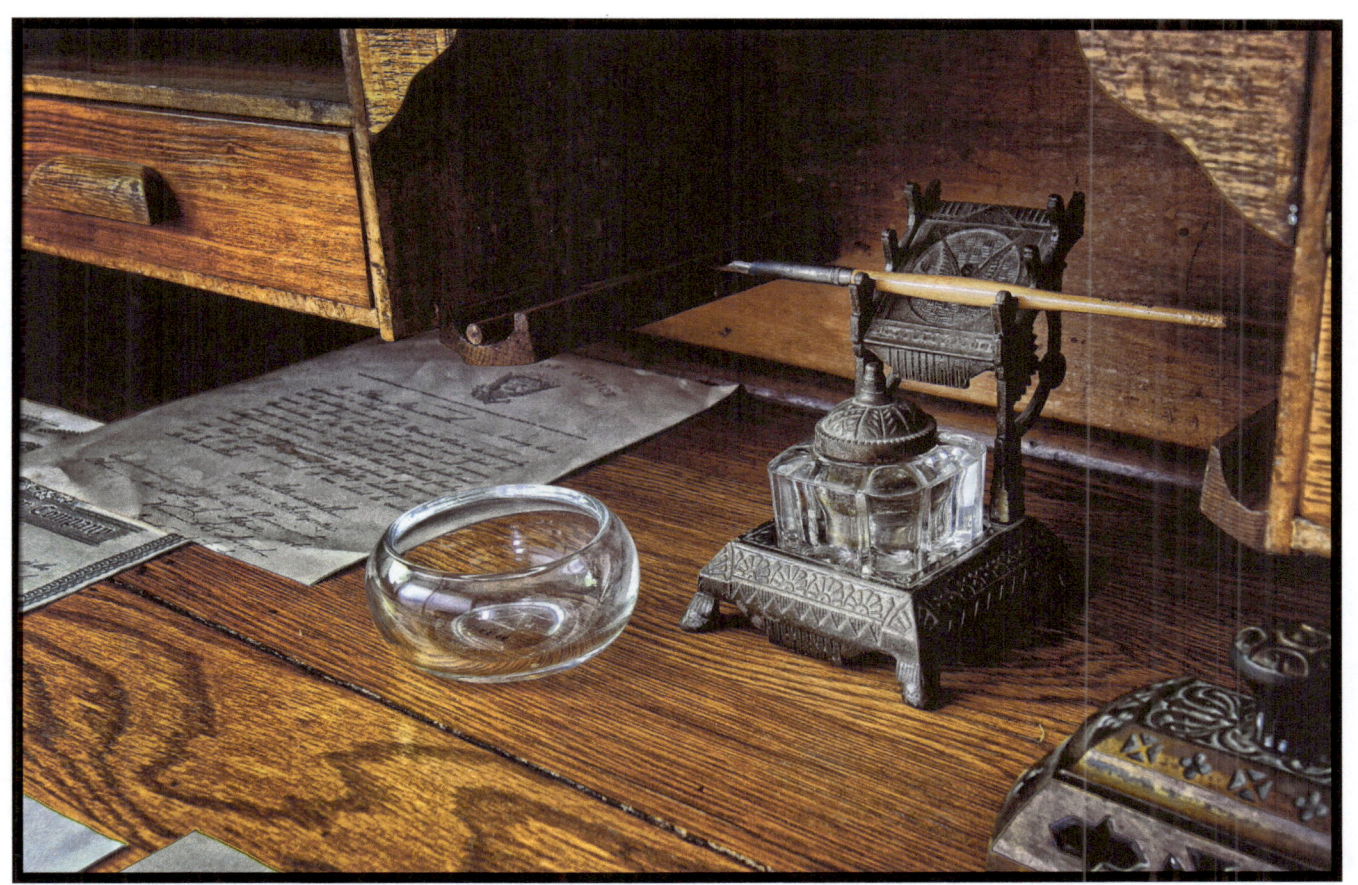

Ink & Pen - Robert Mance

"Colonel Allensworth's exquisite desk where I can see him sitting for hours writing with this ink and pen."

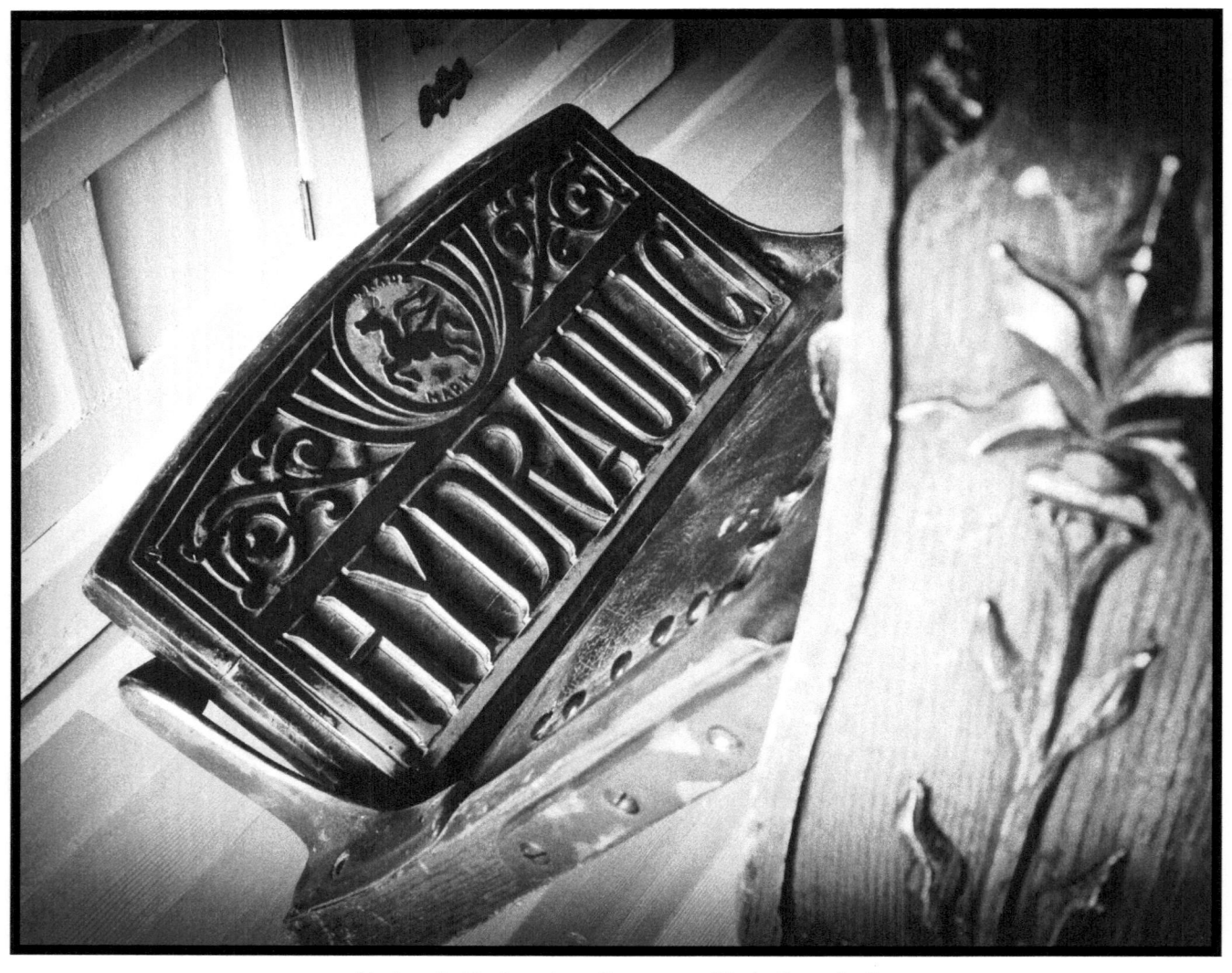

Hydraulic Barbershop Footrest - Clark Campbell

"Detail of the barbershop chair inside of Frank Milner's Barbershop. In its time, the barbershop was a local male hub for the discussion of news, business, and social issues related to the town of Allensworth."

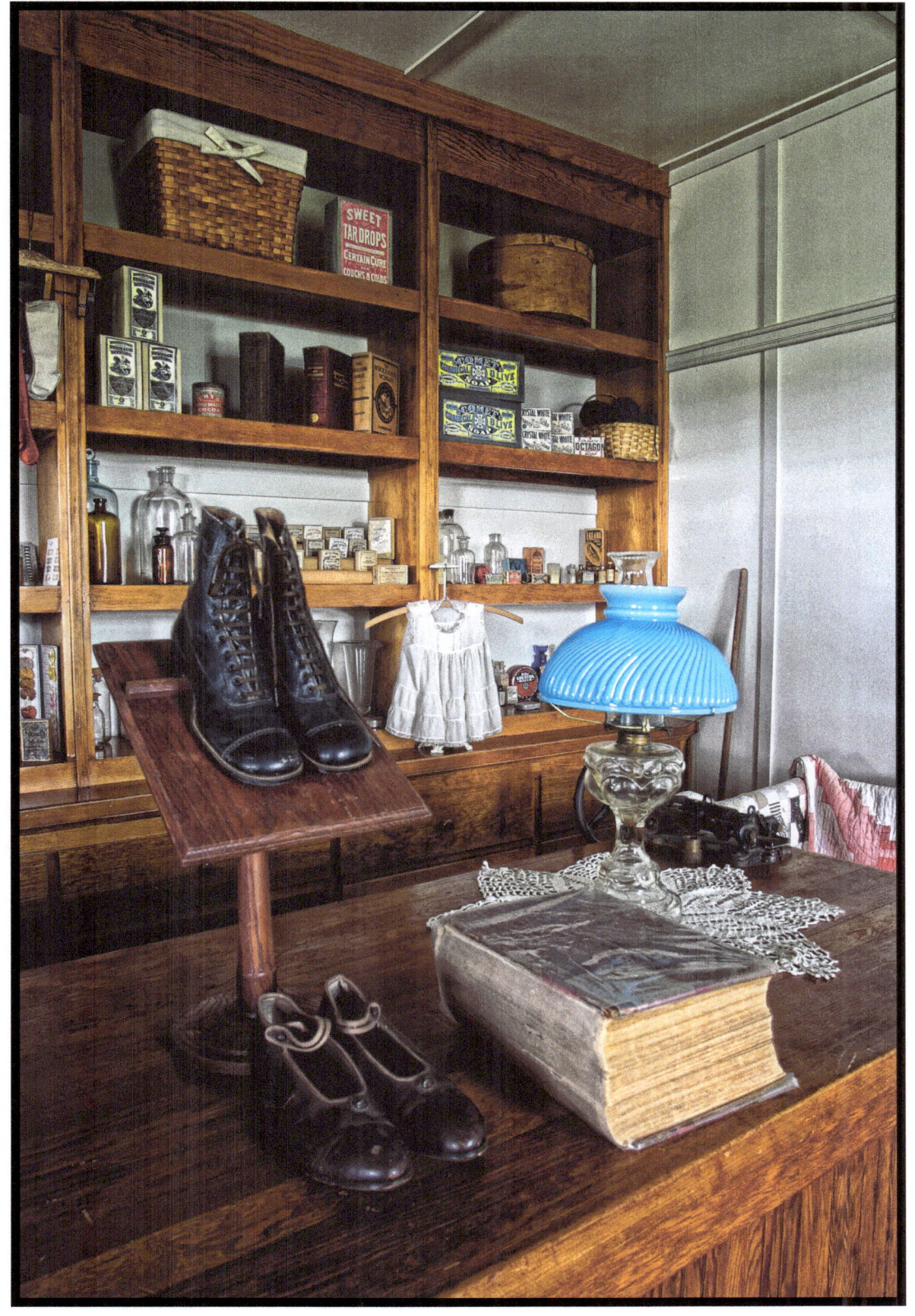

Shoes for Sale - Robert Mance

"A beautiful pair of shoes and other wonderful items for sale at the Scott and Grosse Store."

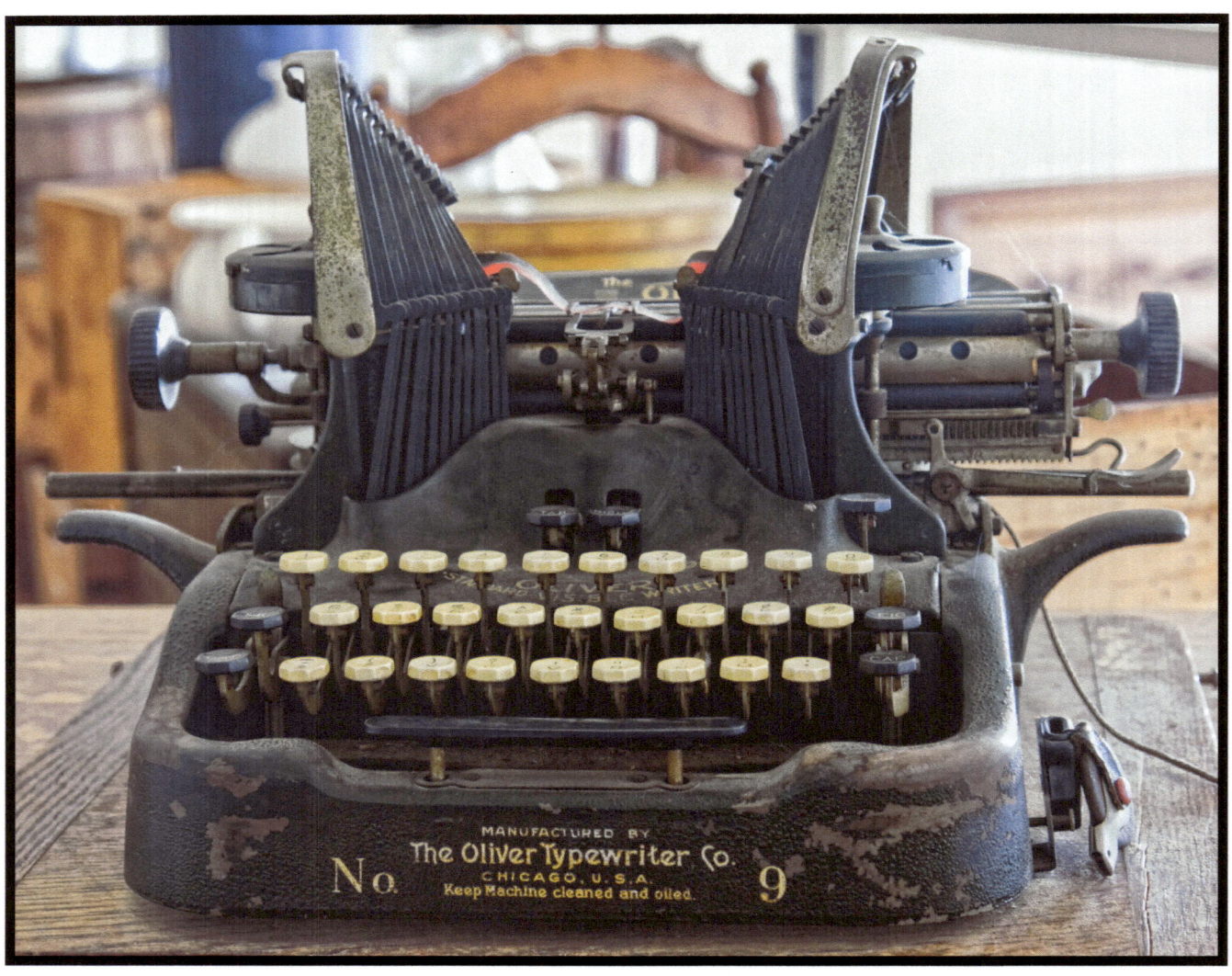

Oliver Typewriter - Hindsman Store - Jean Carter

"Located in the loft of the Hindsman Store, where steep stairs lead up to a treasure trove of finds to photograph."

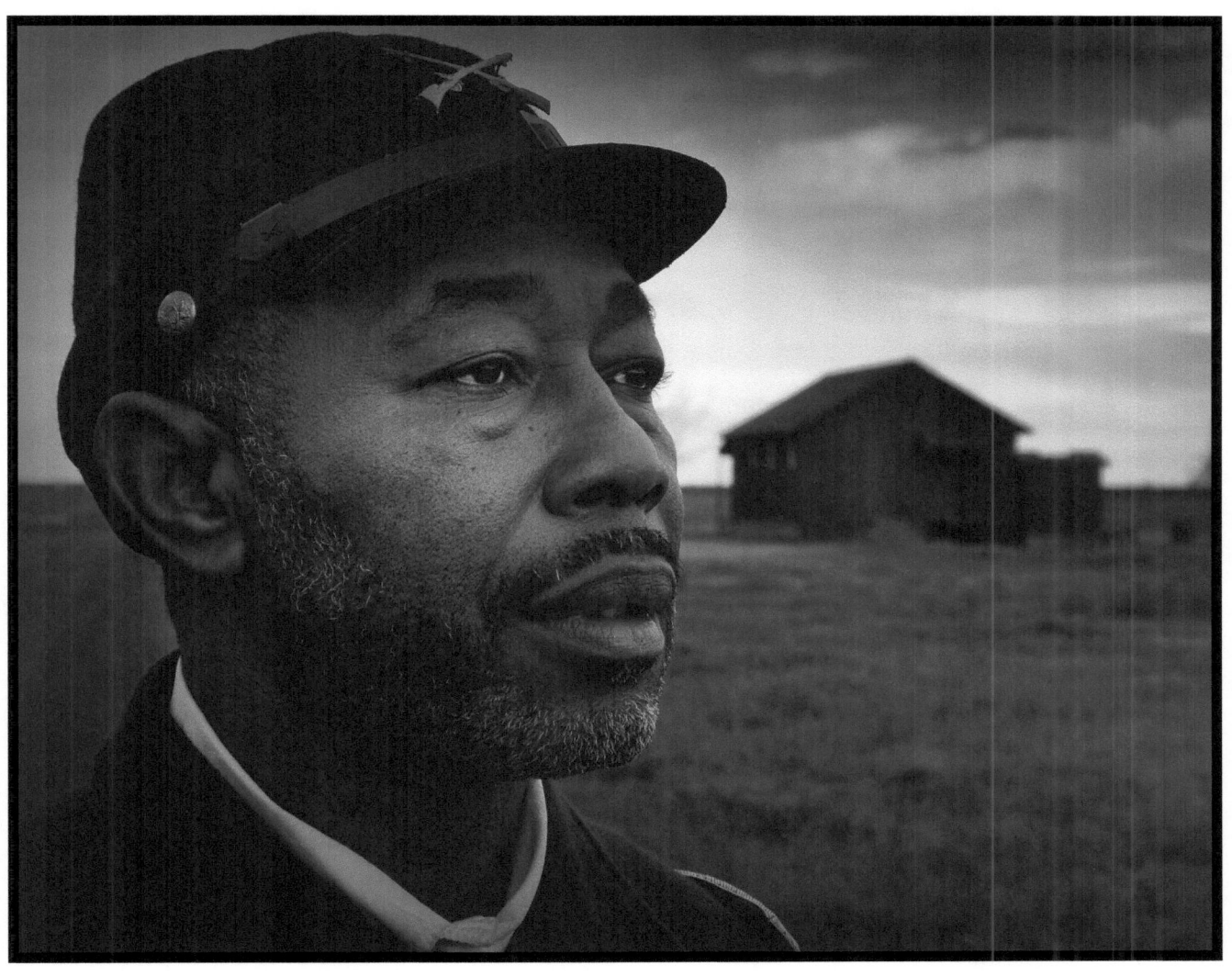

Emmett Harden, Buffalo Soldier, Allensworth State Park - Clark Campbell

'A docent at the park, Mr. Harden helps to educate and inform visitors of the history and importance of Colonel Allensworth State Historic Park."

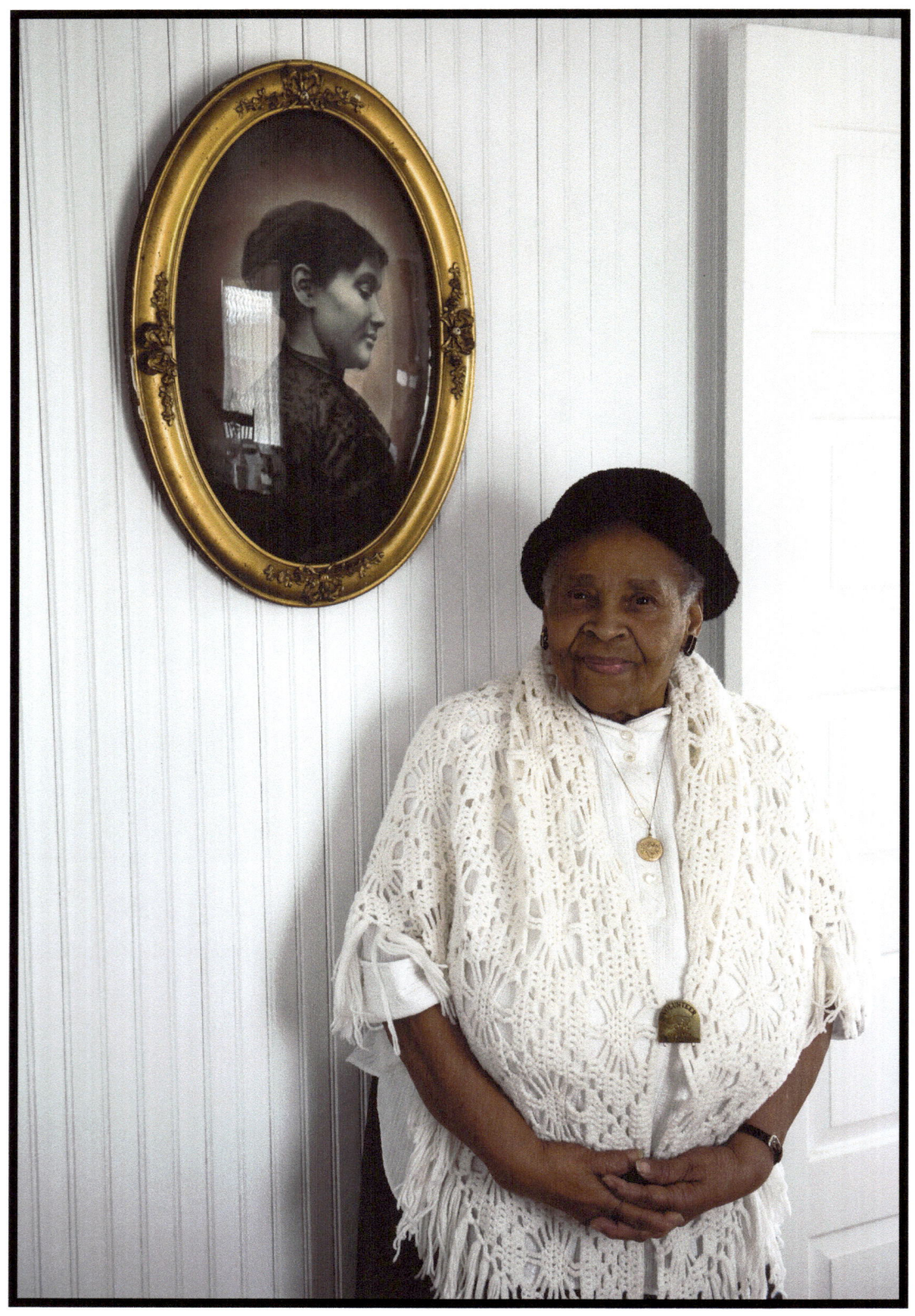

Mrs. Alice Royal – Christy Stallcup

"This photograph was taken in the Hackett home where Mrs. Alice Royal was born in 1923. Mr. James and Mrs. Alice Hackett were her maternal grandparents. She is standing next to a photograph of her grandmother."

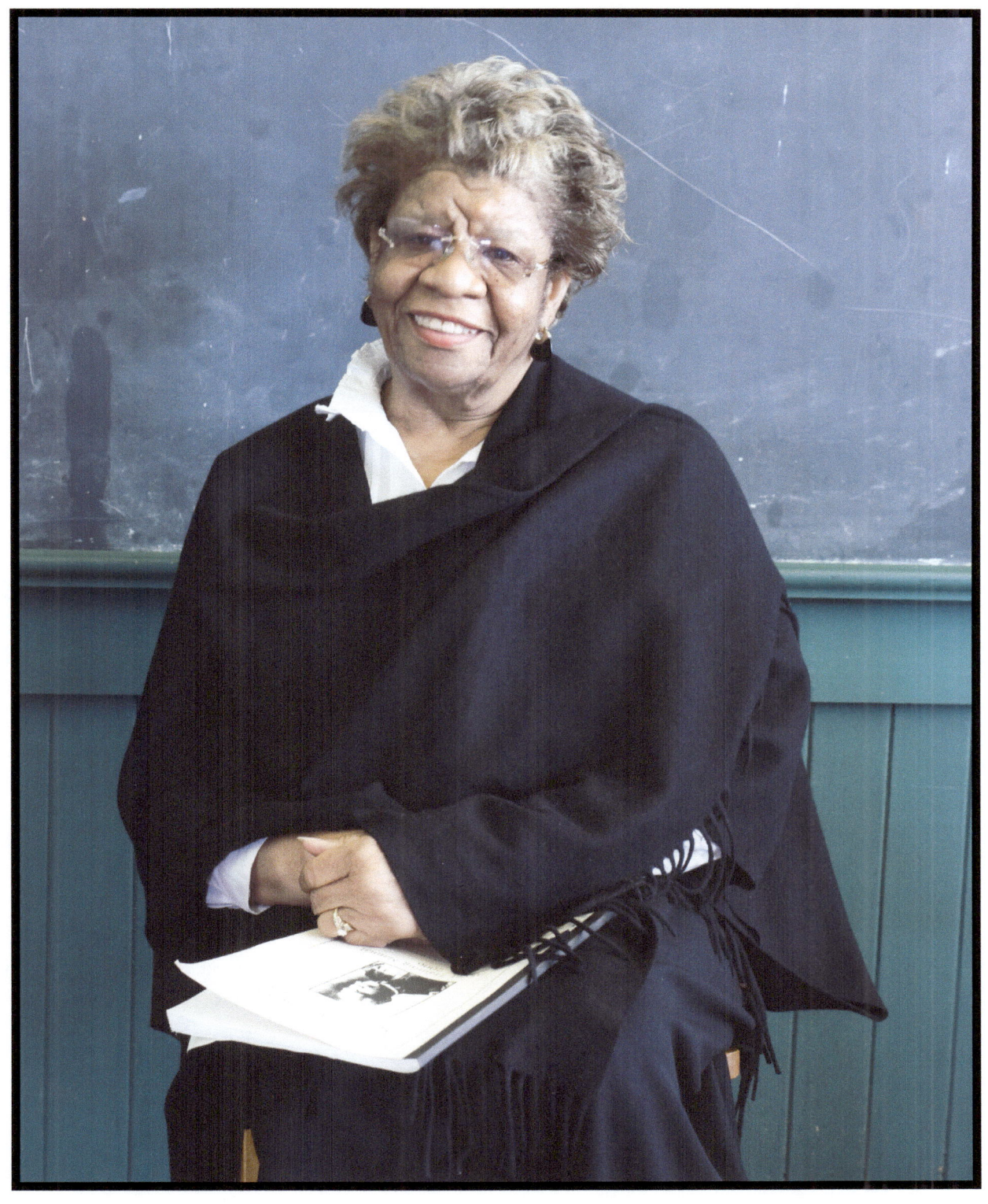

School Teacher - Amanda Moore - Jean Carter

"Amanda Moore, docent, of the Allensworth Elementary Schoolhouse, also taught class there."

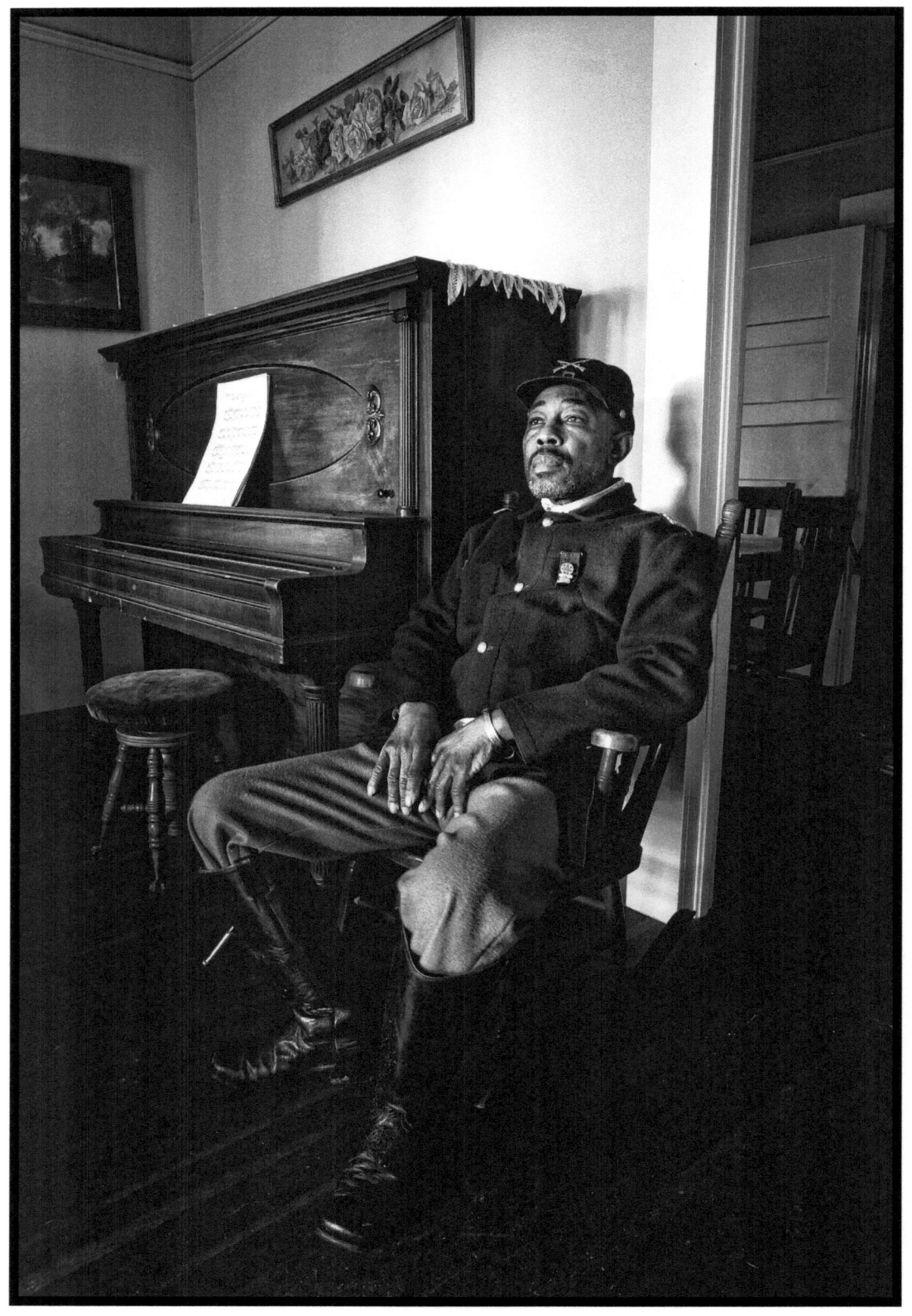

Standing Guard - Robert Mance

"Emmett Harden watching over the Smith House, and volunteering his time as one of the wonderful docents."

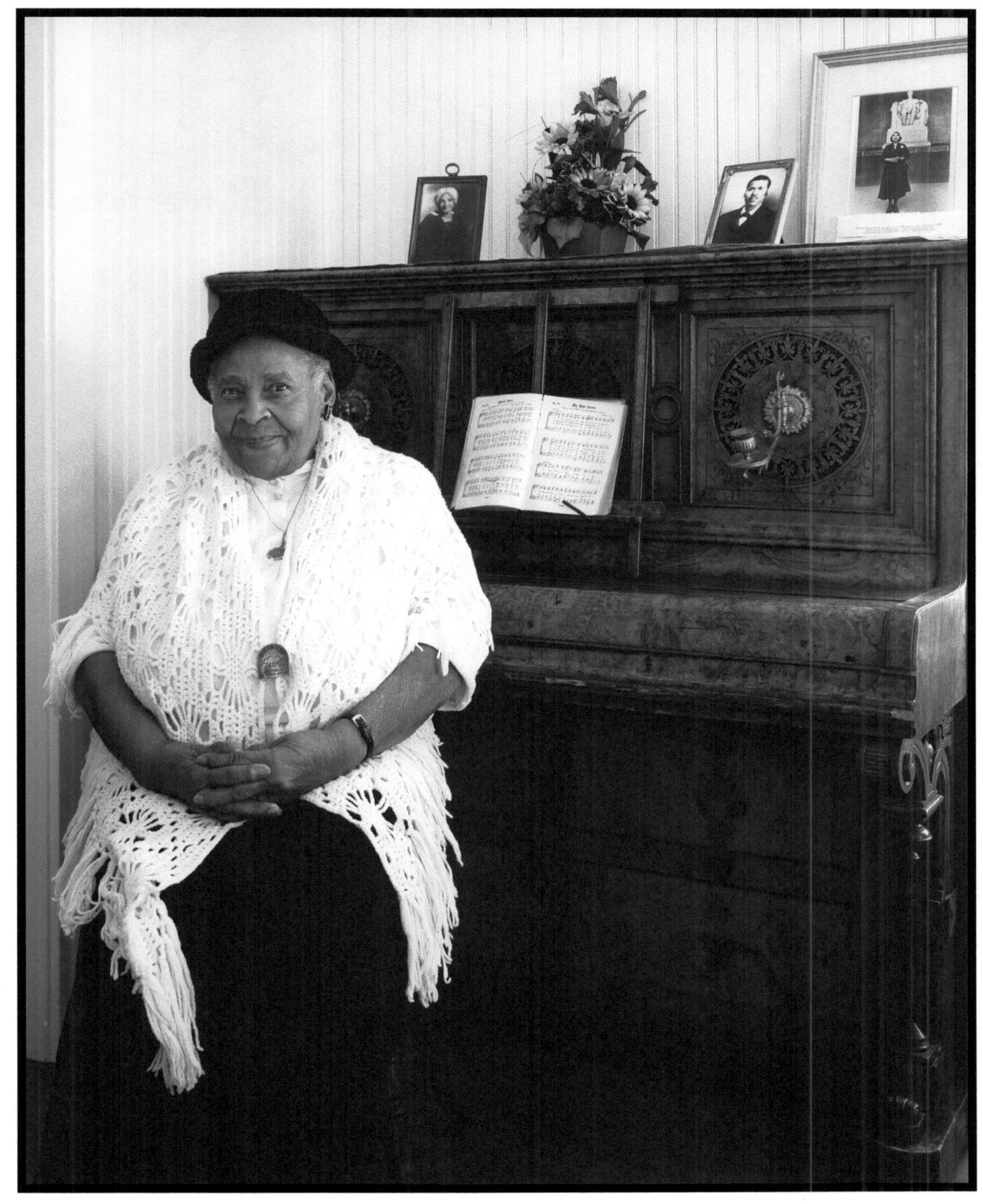

Alice Royal Portrait - Rick Russell

"Photograph of Alice Royal, in the parlor of Hackett House, where she lived as a child."

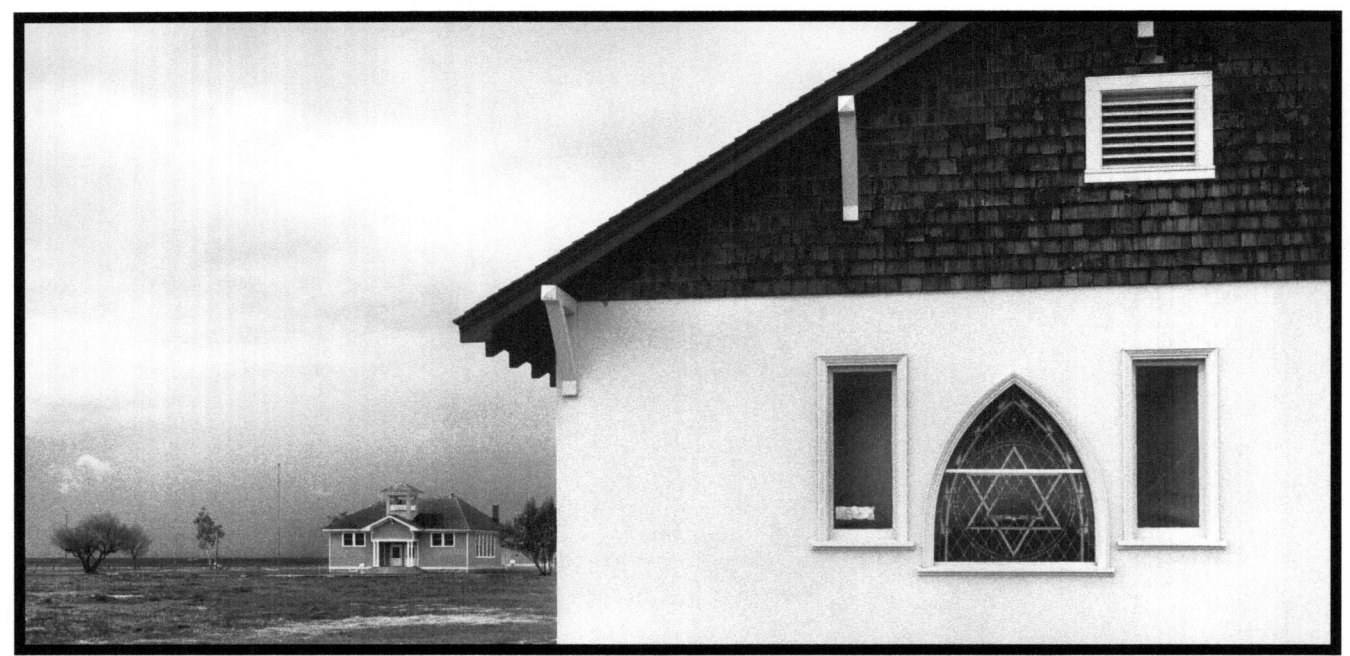

Baptist Church - Ted Dayton

"Construction of the town's Baptist church was begun by Colonel Allensworth and dedicated in 1916, eighteen months after his death. The stained glass window is known as the "Creator's Star." Visible in the distance is the Allensworth Schoolhouse, built in 1912."

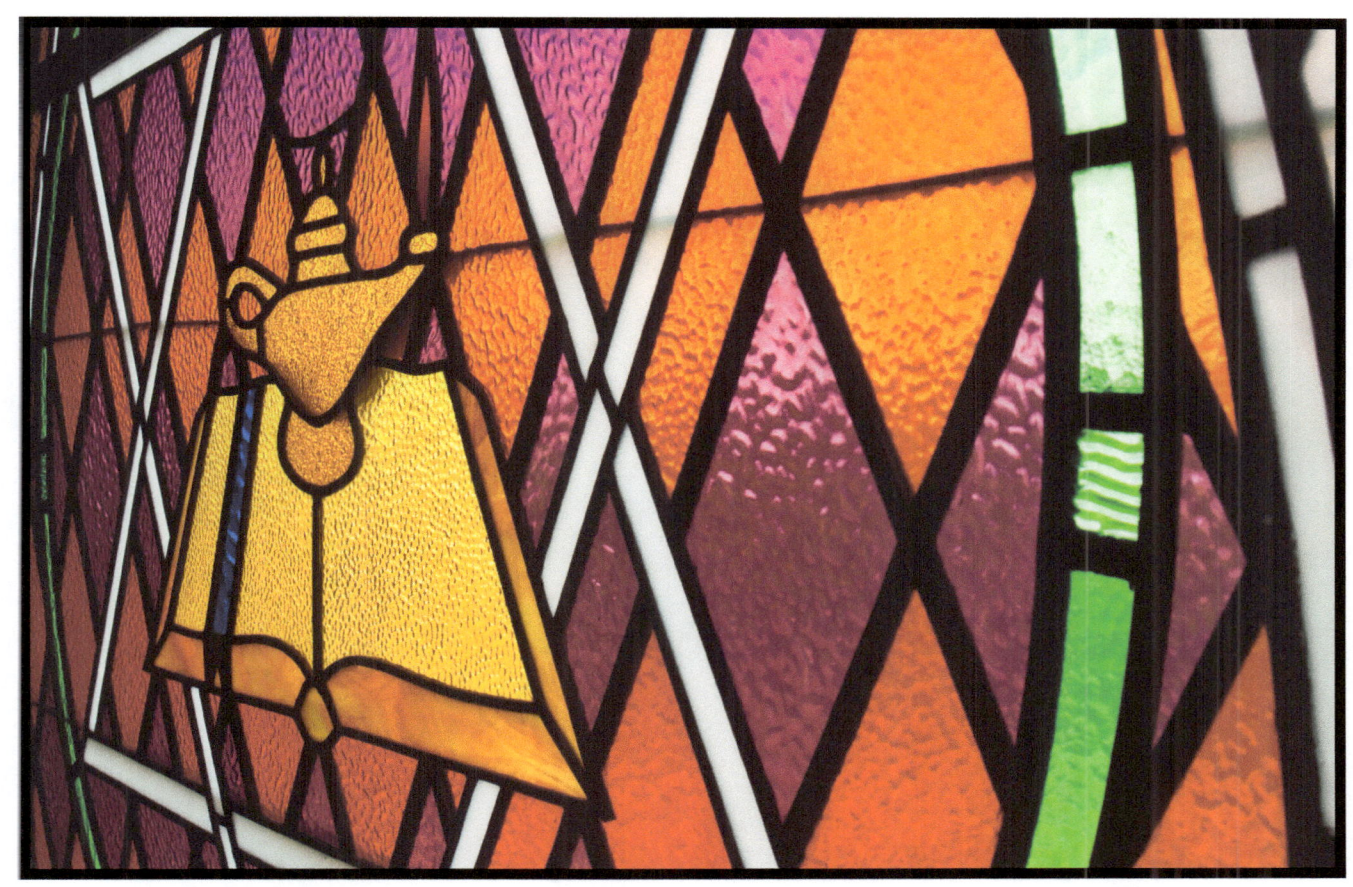

Sacred Stained Glass - Clark Campbell

"Located inside the Baptist church at Allensworth, which sits on property donated by Colonel Allensworth. This reconstruction incorporates pieces of glass from the original stained glass design."

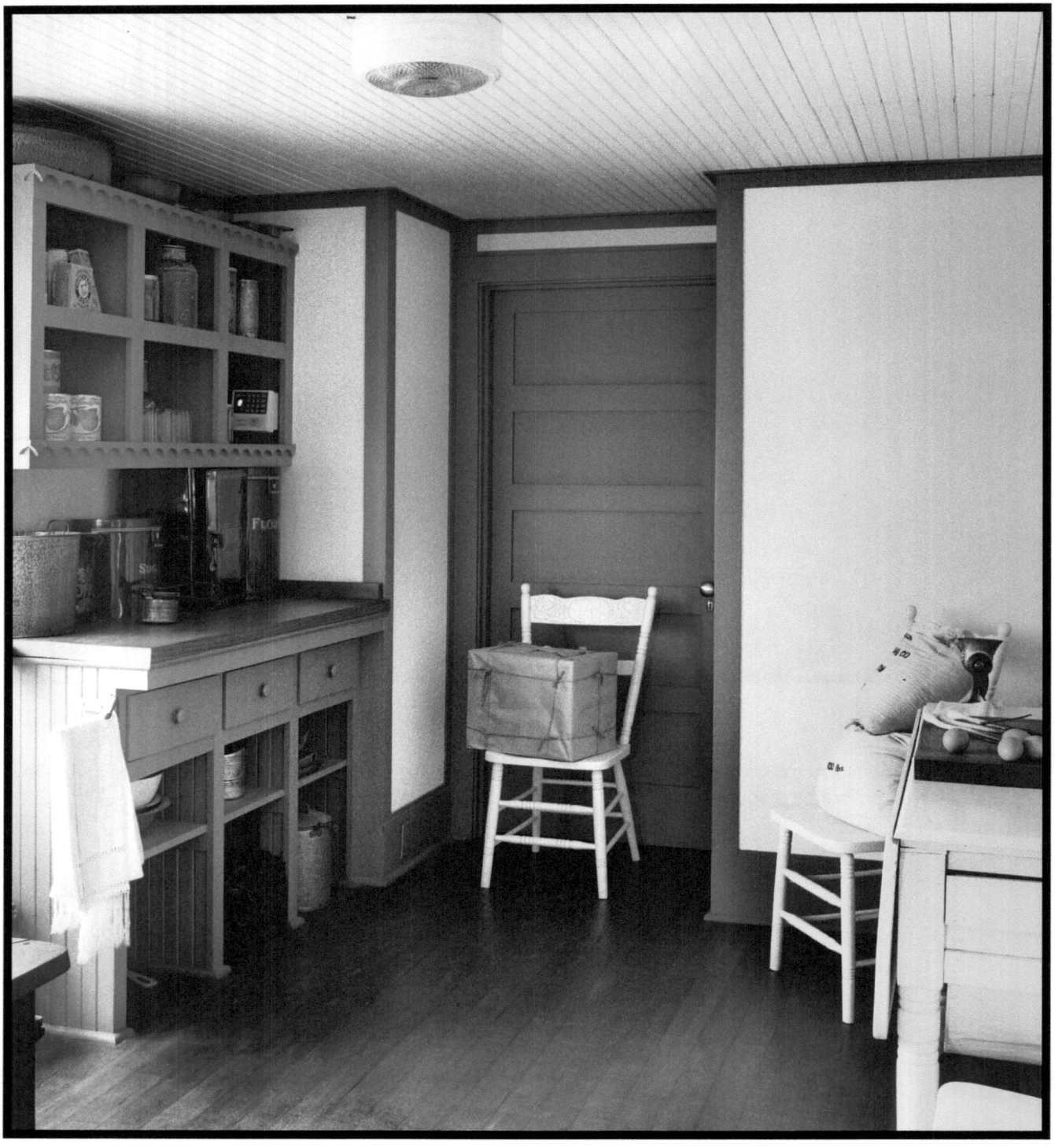

The Kitchen, Colonel Allensworth's Home - Ted Dayton

"This view of Allensworth's kitchen is toward the door leading to his bedroom. If you look closely at the shelving above the counter, you can see a modern security alarm panel. The window just outside the left edge of this photo faces west, into Colonel Allensworth's back yard. Note the low ceilings, just barely above the door frame."

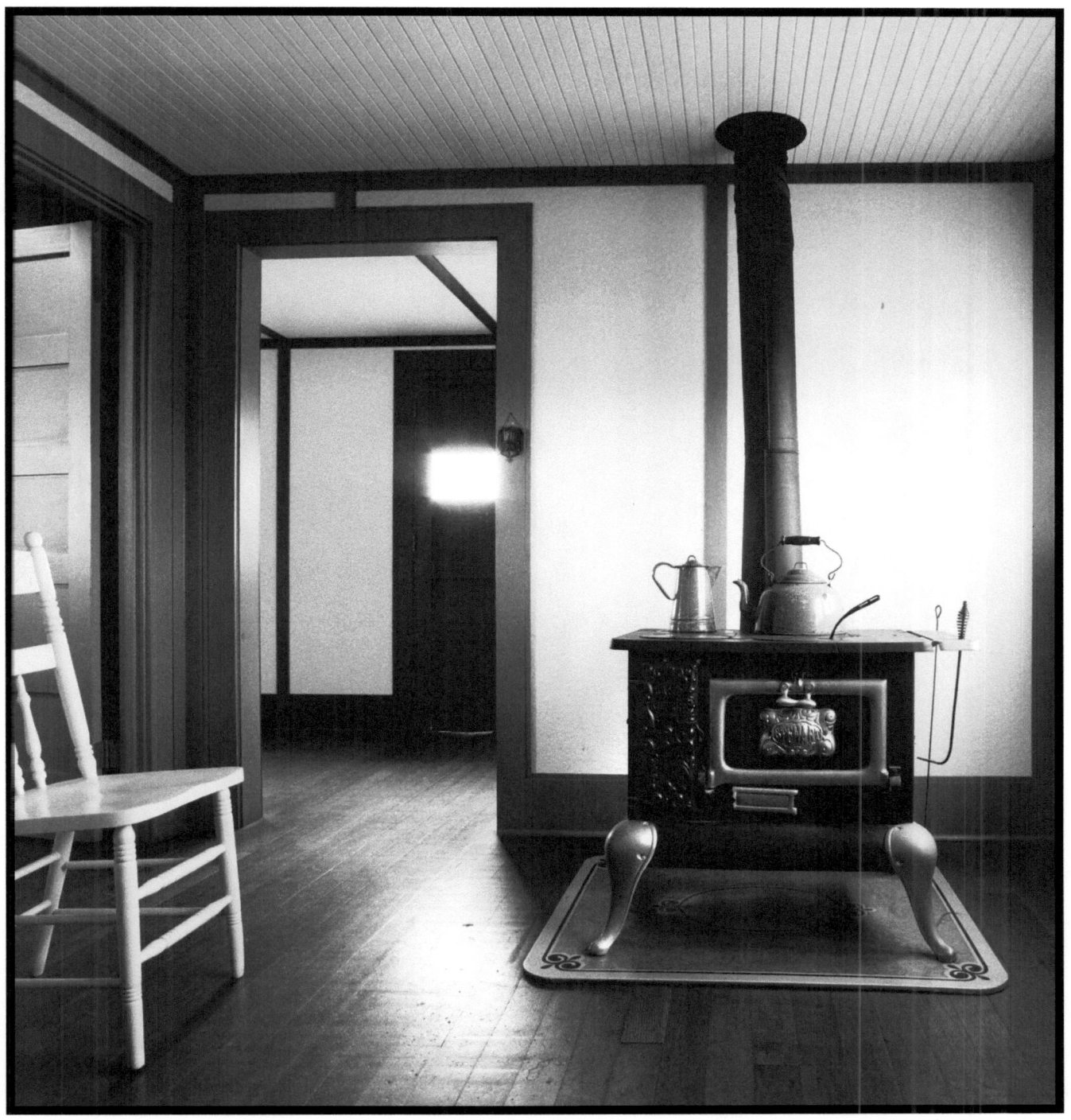

The Kitchen, Colonel Allensworth's Home - Ted Dayton

"This photo, taken from the doorway to Colonel Allensworth's bedroom, shows the wood-burning stove next to the only kitchen window. Note the lack of working space or a table for meals. The doorway to the left leads to a formal dining room; through the door beyond the stove and to the left is the Colonel's personal desk. The door in the distance leads outside, to the south side of the house."

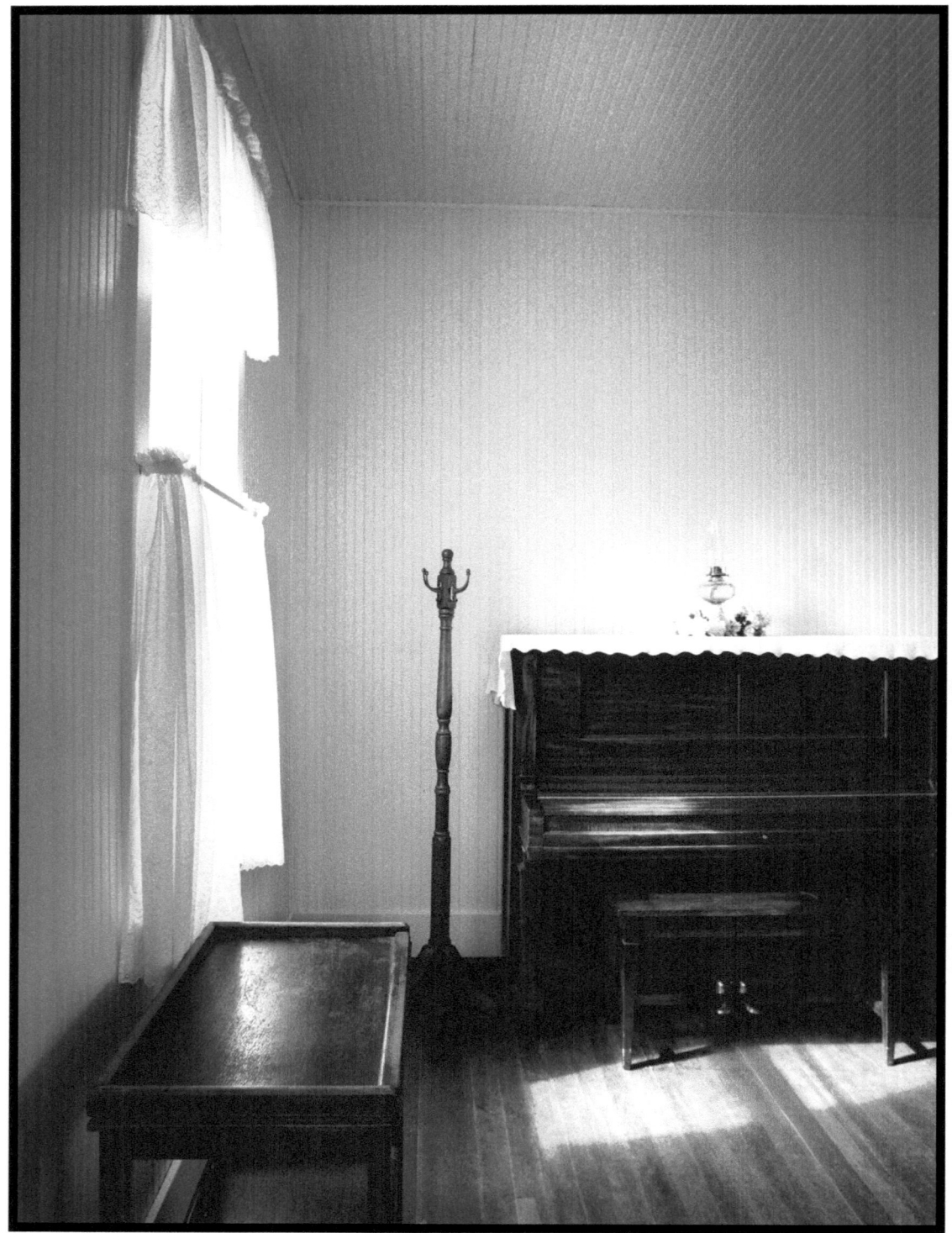

Hotel Dining Room - Ted Dayton

"This upright piano sits in the corner of the hotel's dining room, a large, rectangular room in the center of the hotel, with windows on two sides. With hardwood floors and high ceilings, I imagine booming acoustics. This dining room includes roughly six circular oak tables with several chairs each. Along one wall is a single door leading to a hallway and the hotel's eight guest rooms, which cost 75 cents a night. Along the opposite wall, near the piano, is another door leading to a large kitchen at the rear of the hotel."

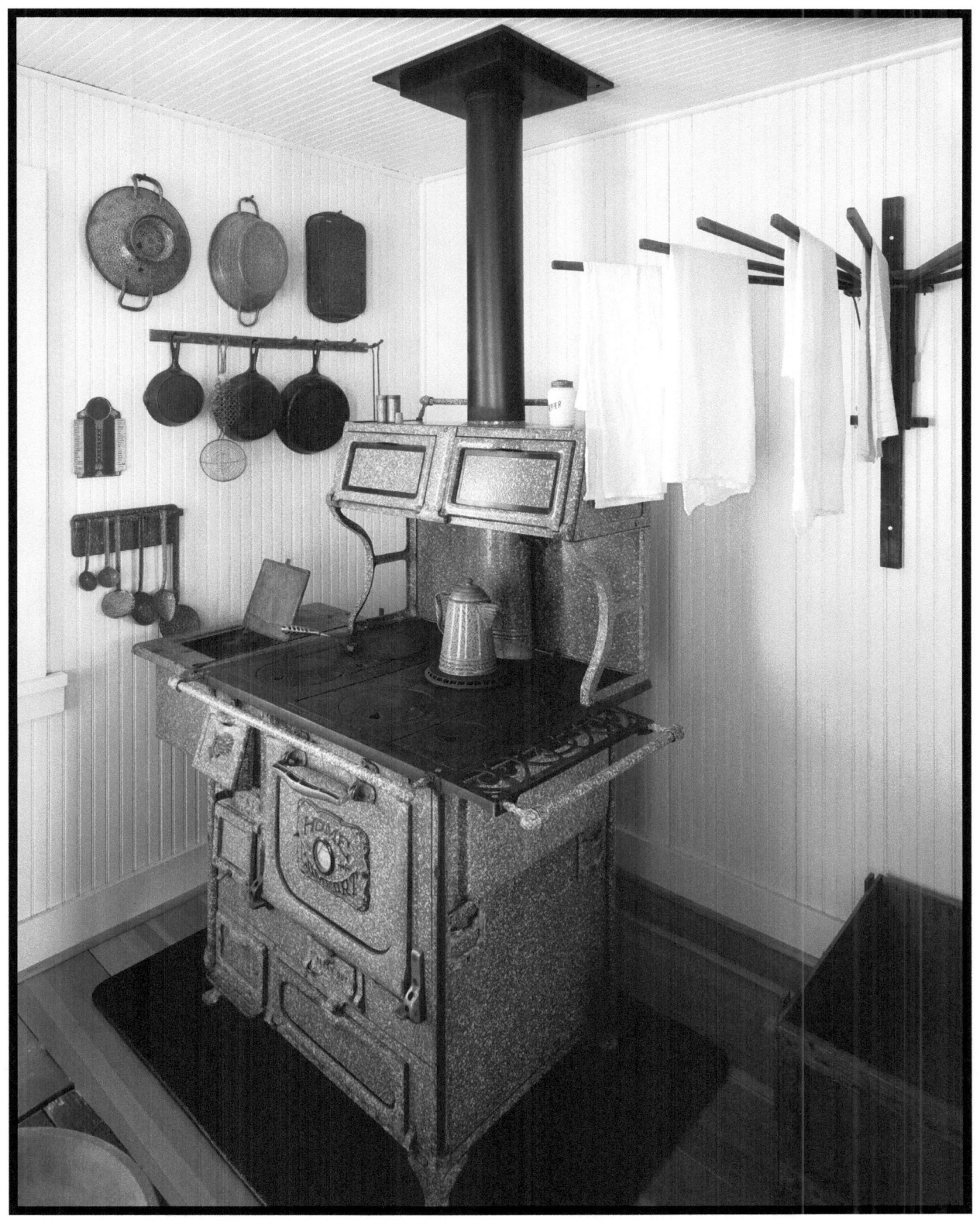

Dodson House and Restaurant Kitchen - Rick Russell

"The kitchen in the Dotson family home and restaurant, the large main room has tables and chairs for customers."

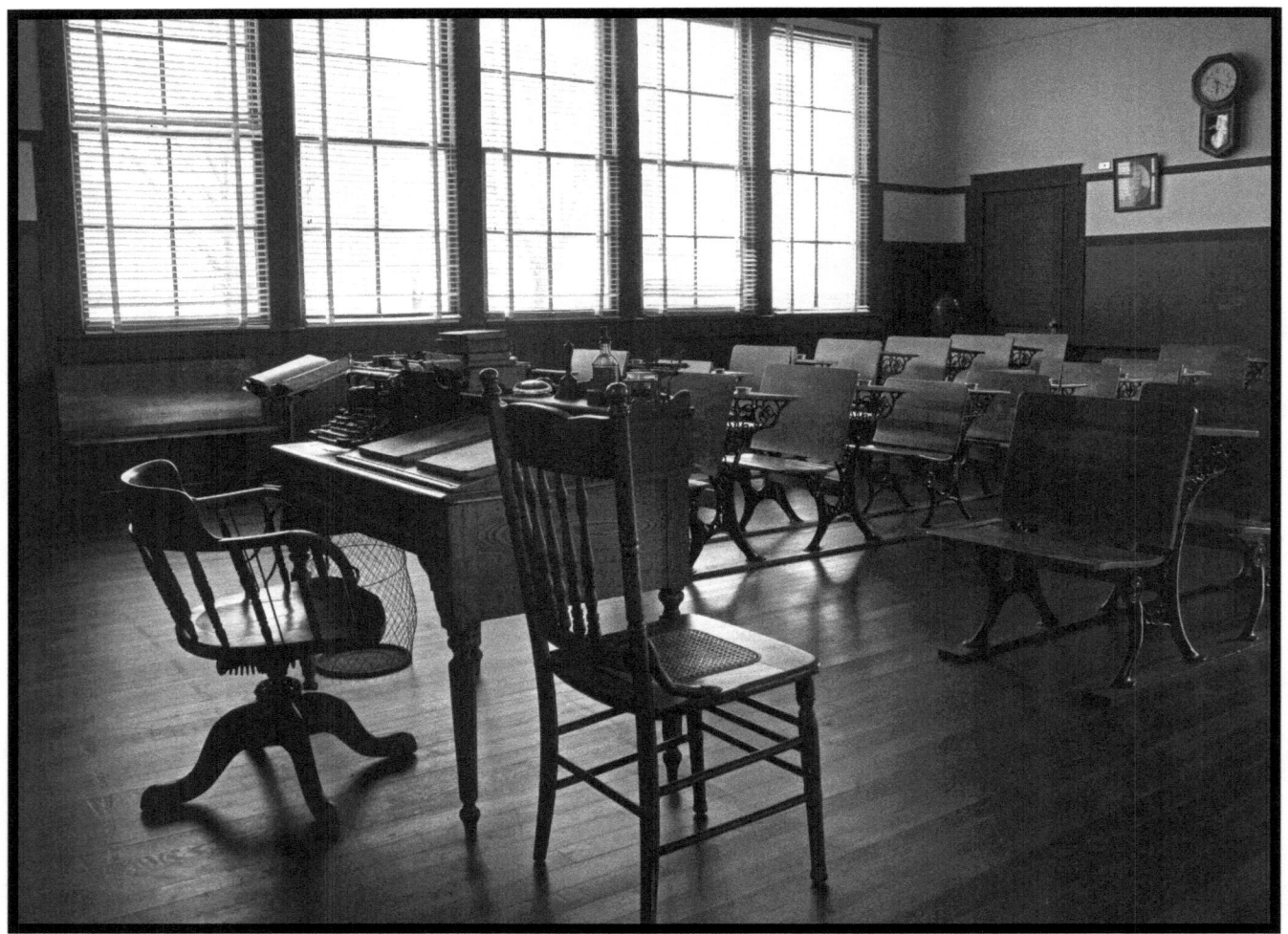

Schoolroom - April Bielefeldt

"Built in 1912, the Allensworth Schoolhouse is impressive, and by some accounts it is the largest building in town. The schoolhouse was considered the best in the Central Valley at that time with two classrooms, two cloakrooms, two dressing rooms, and a stage. The Schoolhouse served many functions in Allensworth: community center, assembly hall, polling place and church."

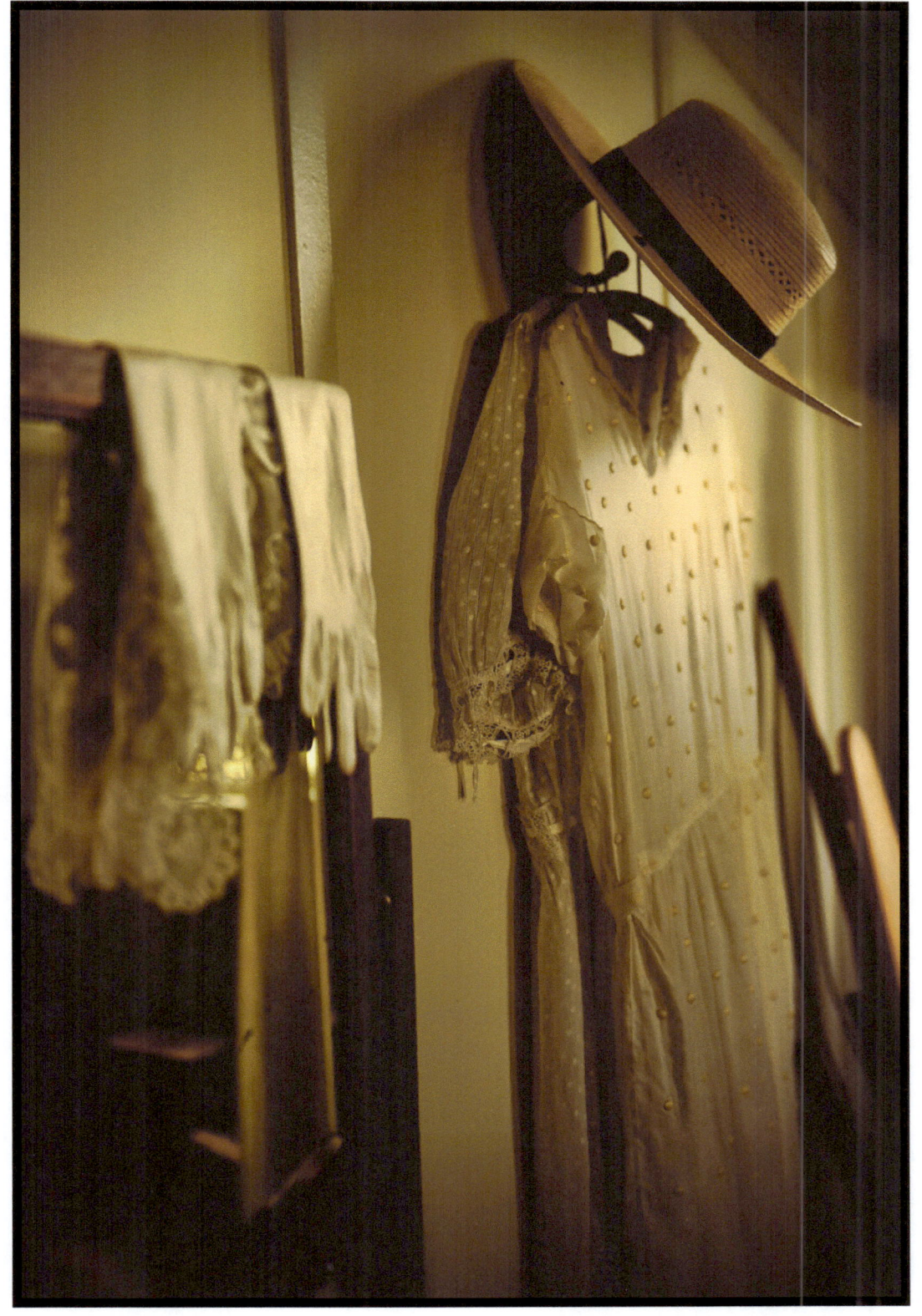

Night Out - Karen Carll

"When I saw this, I imagined a couple long ago, dressing up in their finest for a special cel-ebration."

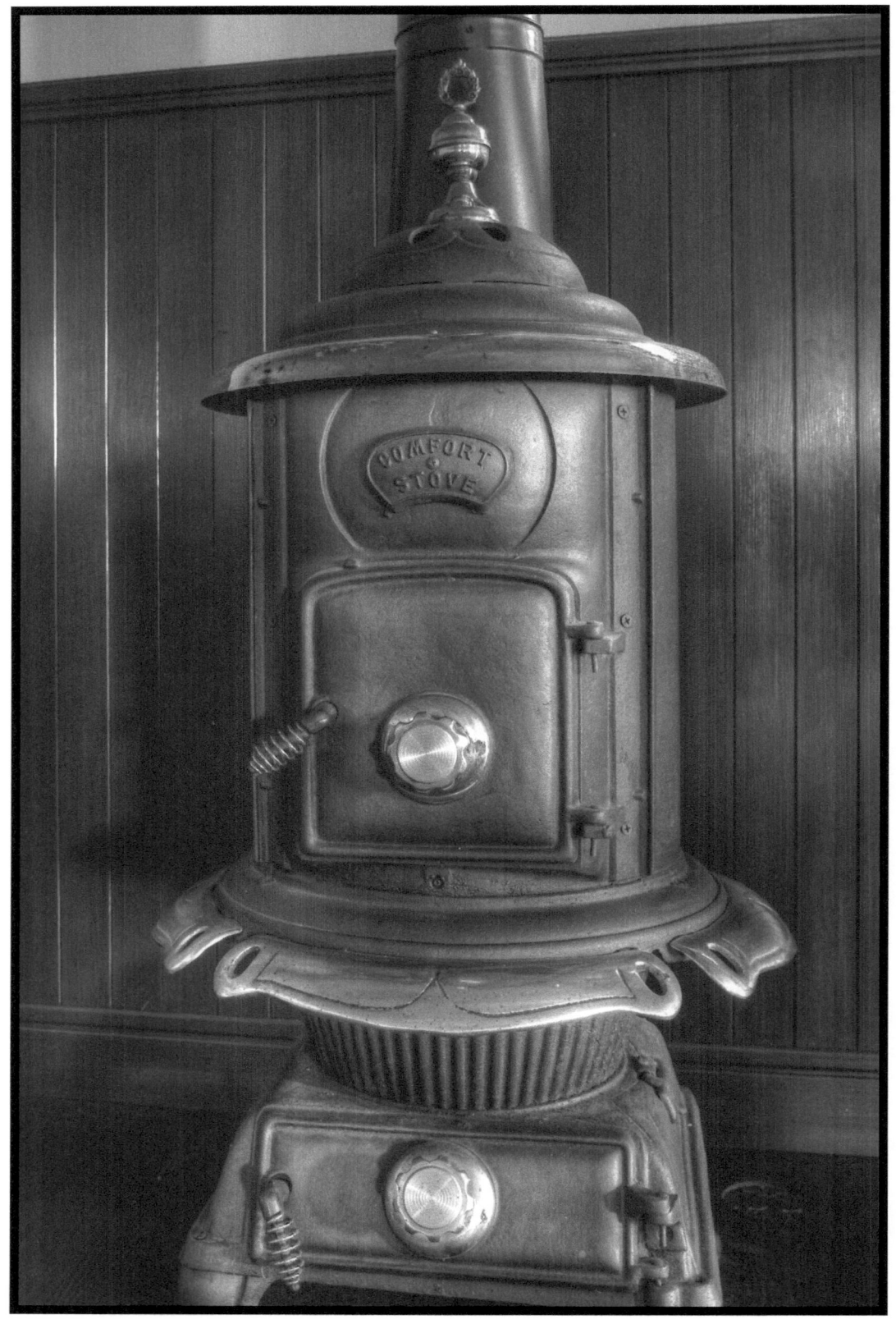

Wood Stove - Mel Carll

"This image just showed tons of character. I could just picture the evening warmth coming from this stove."

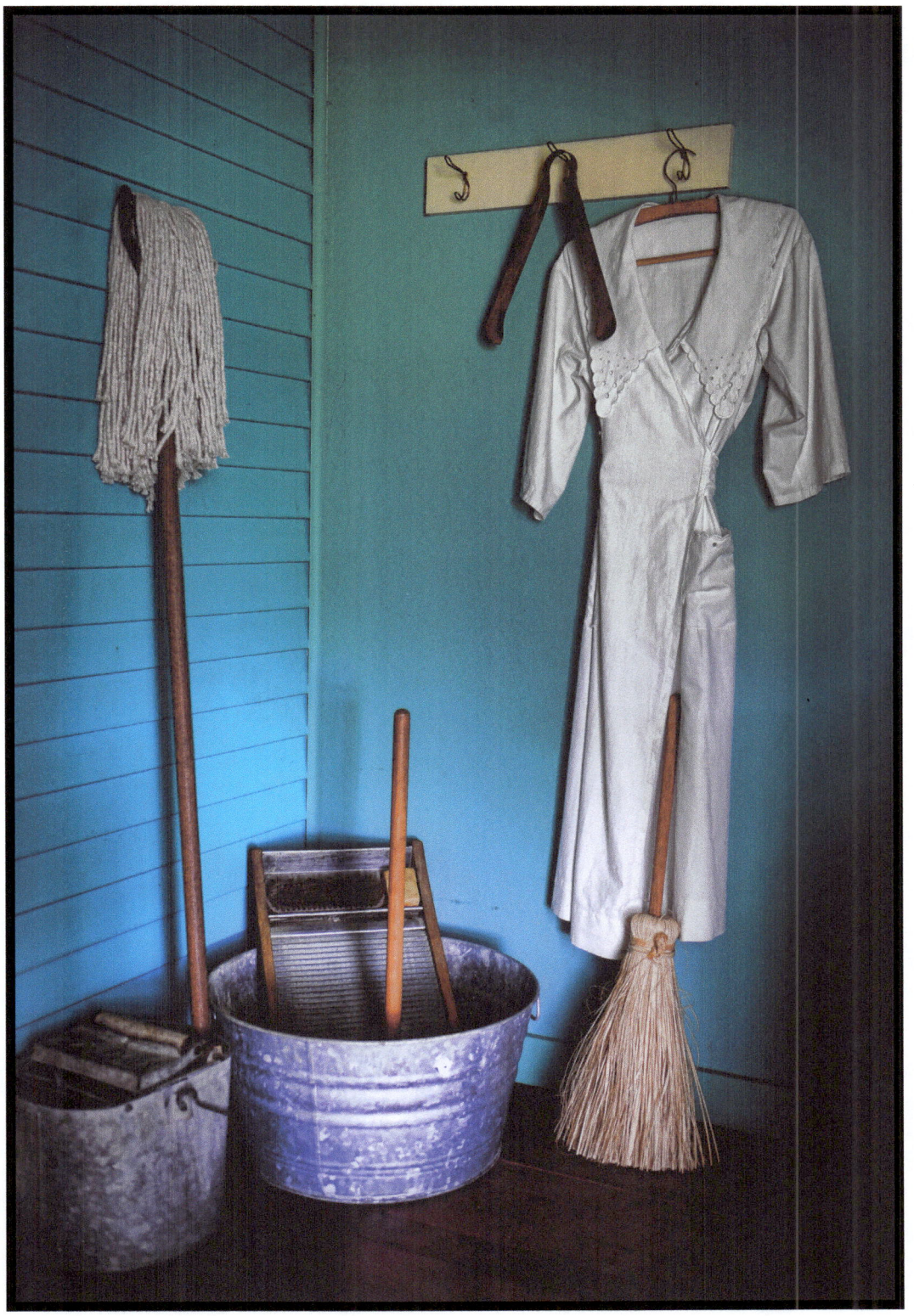

Cleaning Day - Karen Carll

"The way the light brought out the color in this room grabbed my attention. I was also struck by the stark white apron next to the cleaning implements, which speak to me of pride in chores well-done."

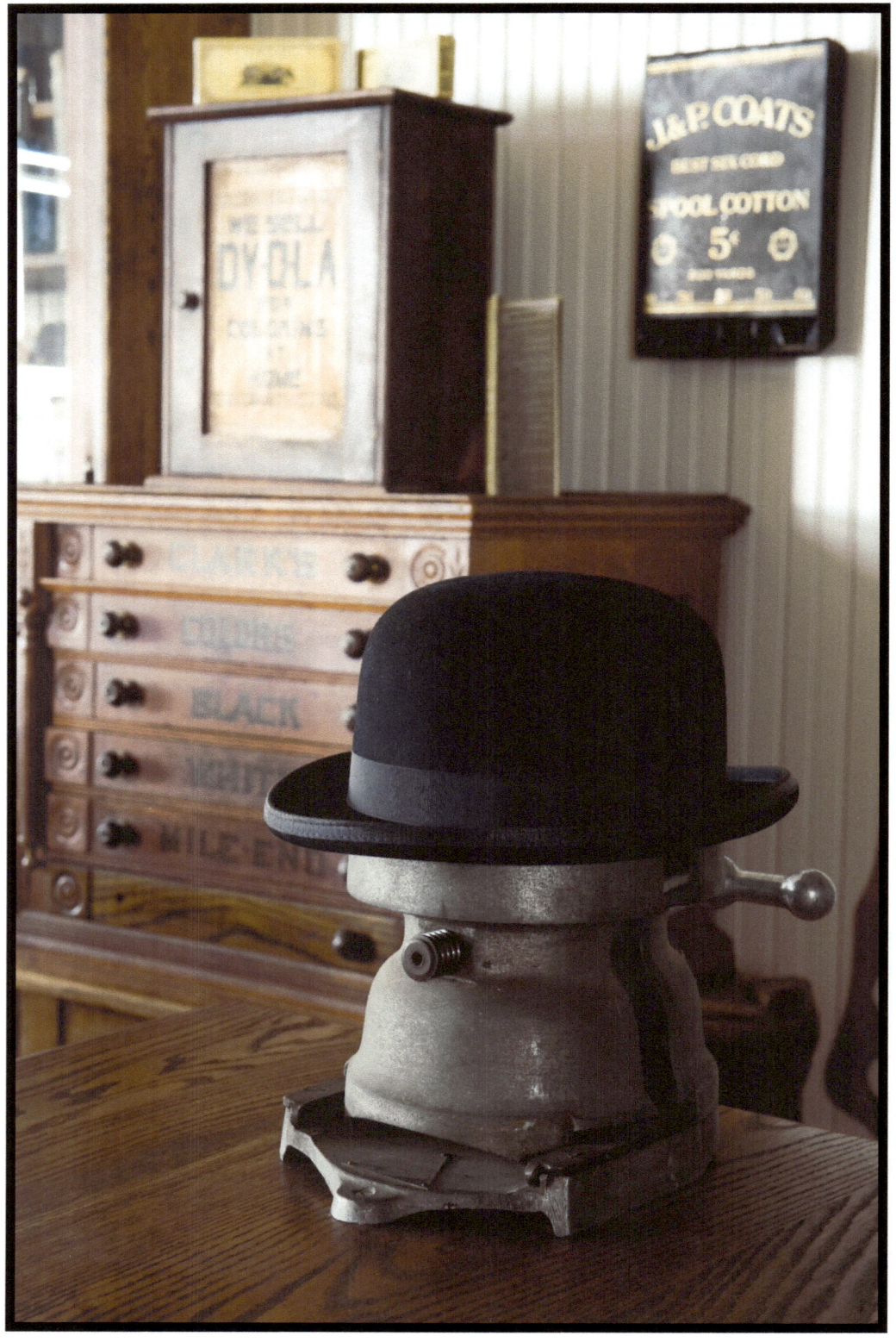

Bowler Hat – Hindsman & Co General Store - Christy Stallcup

"The bowler hat, also known as a coke hat or derby, is a hard felt hat with a rounded crown. This hat sits on a vintage hat stretcher in the general store."

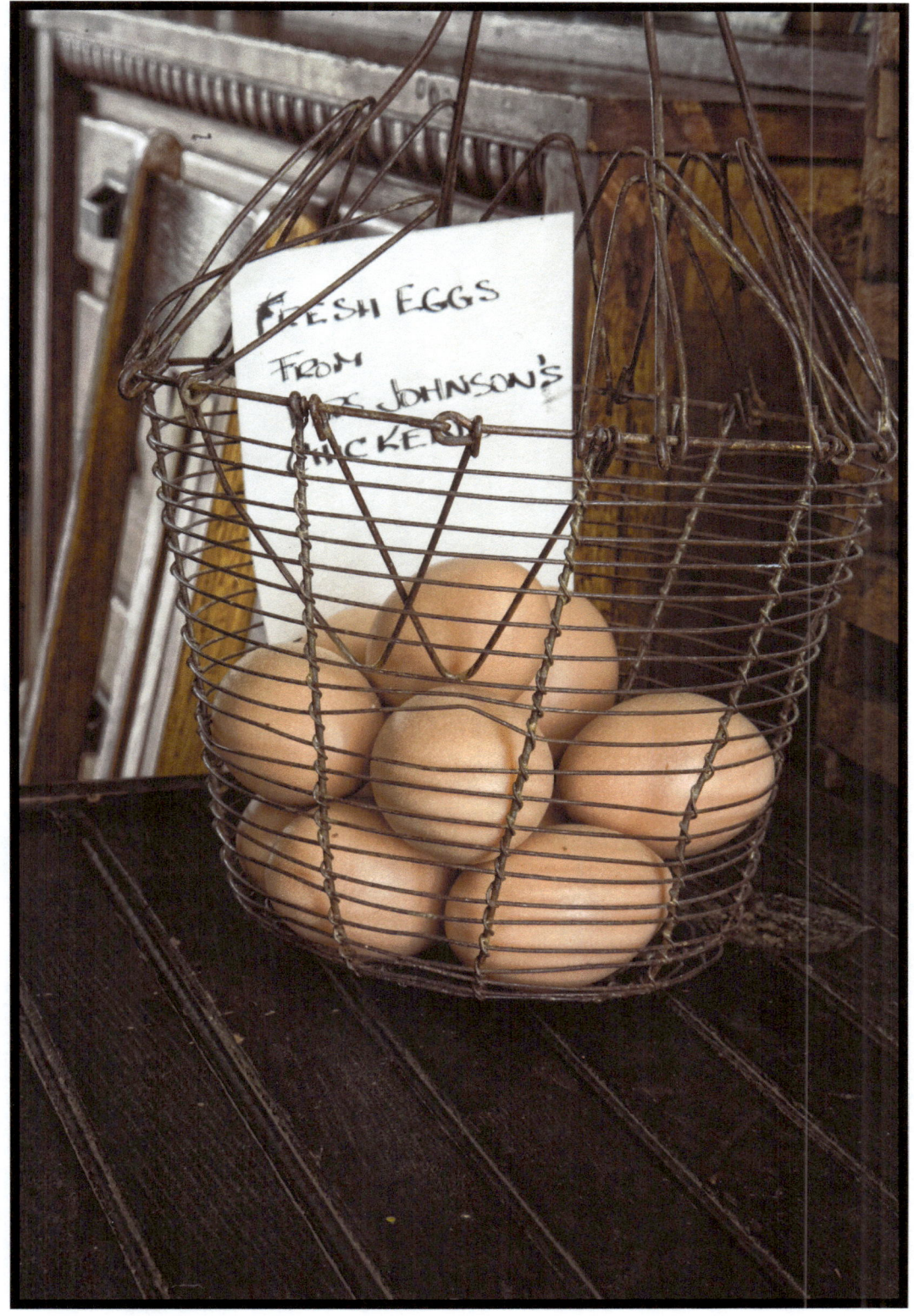

Fresh Eggs for Sale- Hindsman Store - Jean Carter

"Located in the Hindsman Store. Mrs. Johnson brought in a fresh egg basket to sell to the residents of Allensworth. It represents families trying to make a living the best way they knew how."

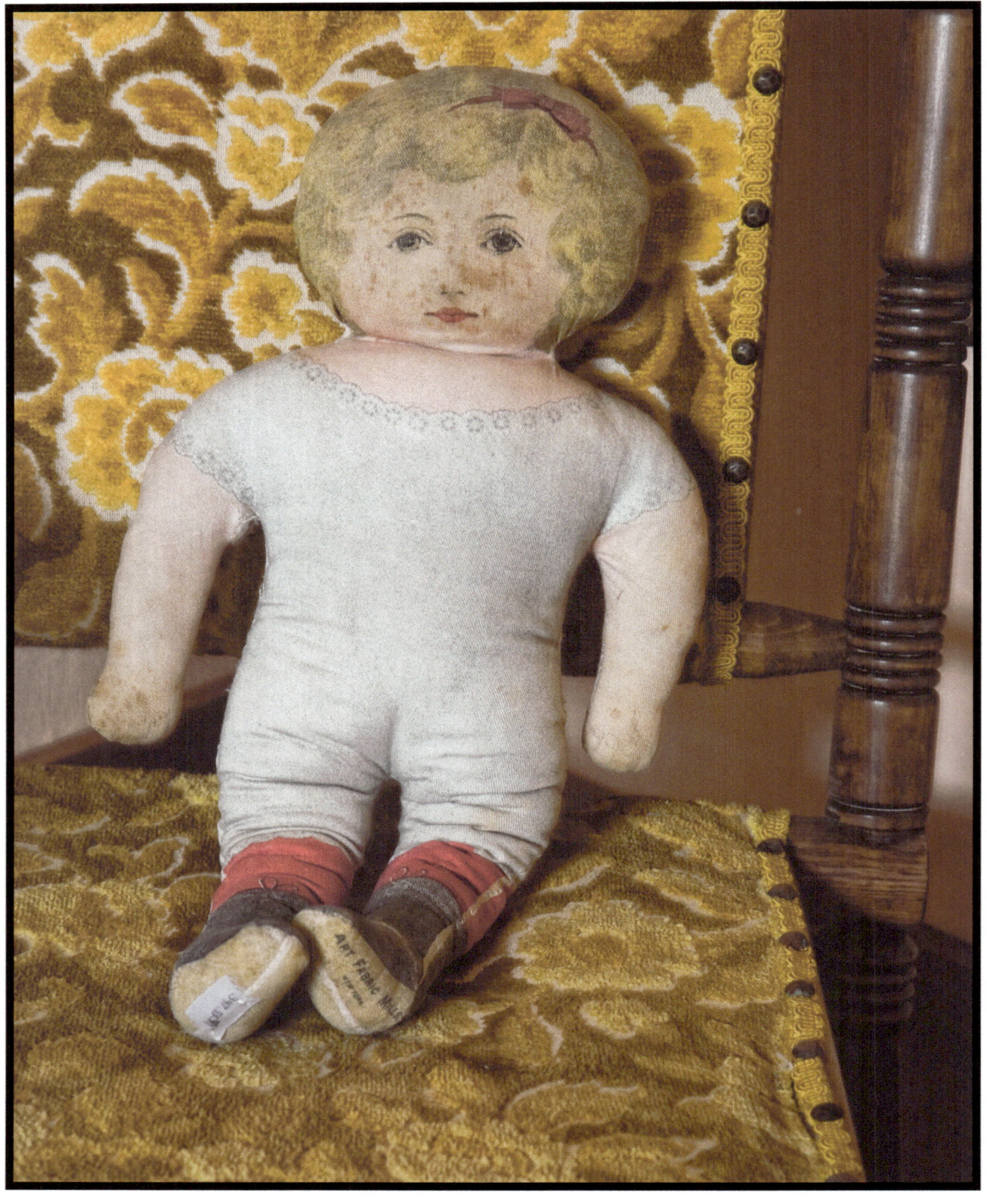

Doll - Hackett House - Jean Carter

"Located in the bedroom of the Hackett House. I can image a little girl playing with this treasured doll."

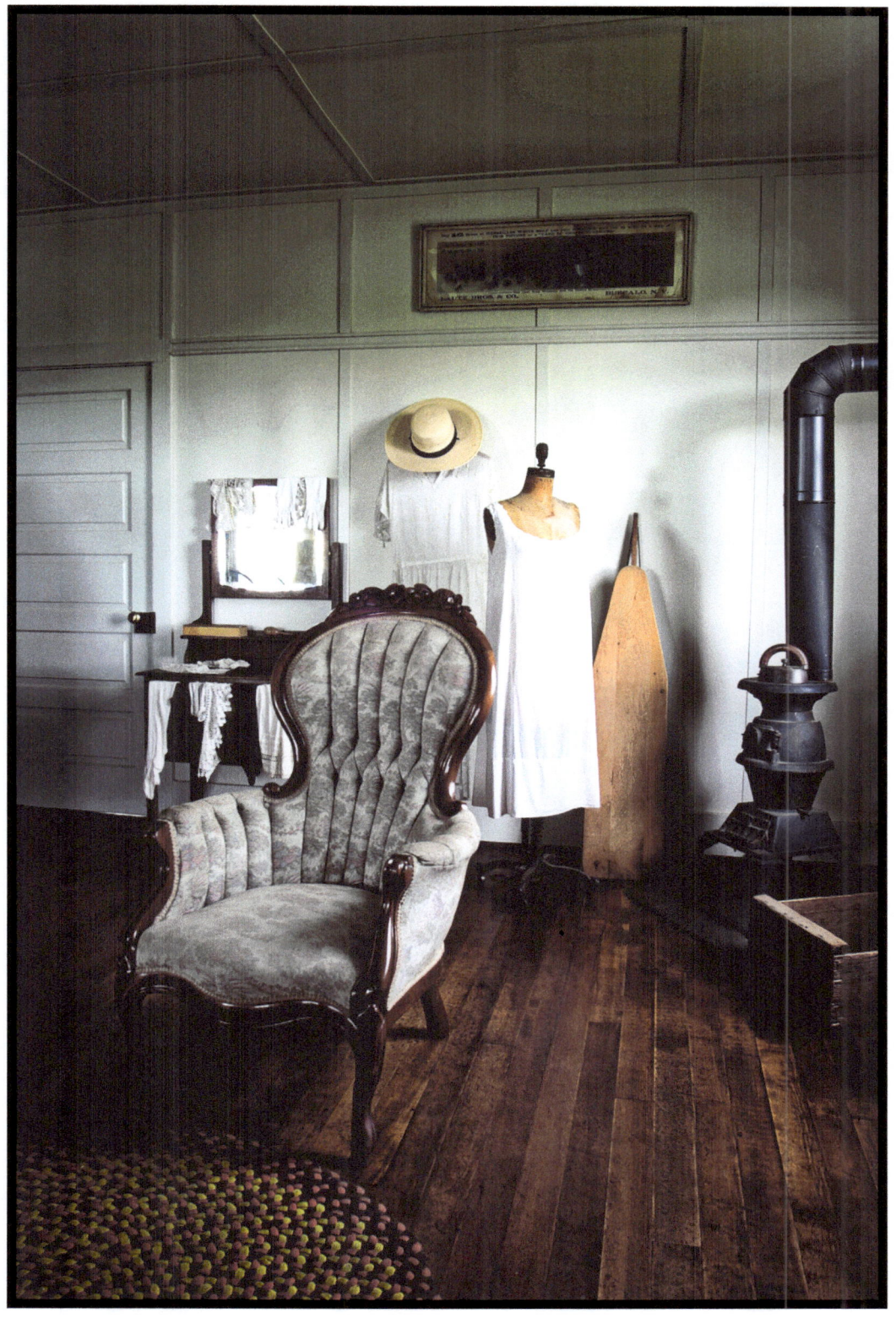

Sit for a Spell - Robert Mance

"After a hard day of shopping I'm sure it was nice to sit by the warmth of the fire and chat with friends at the Scott and Grosse Store."

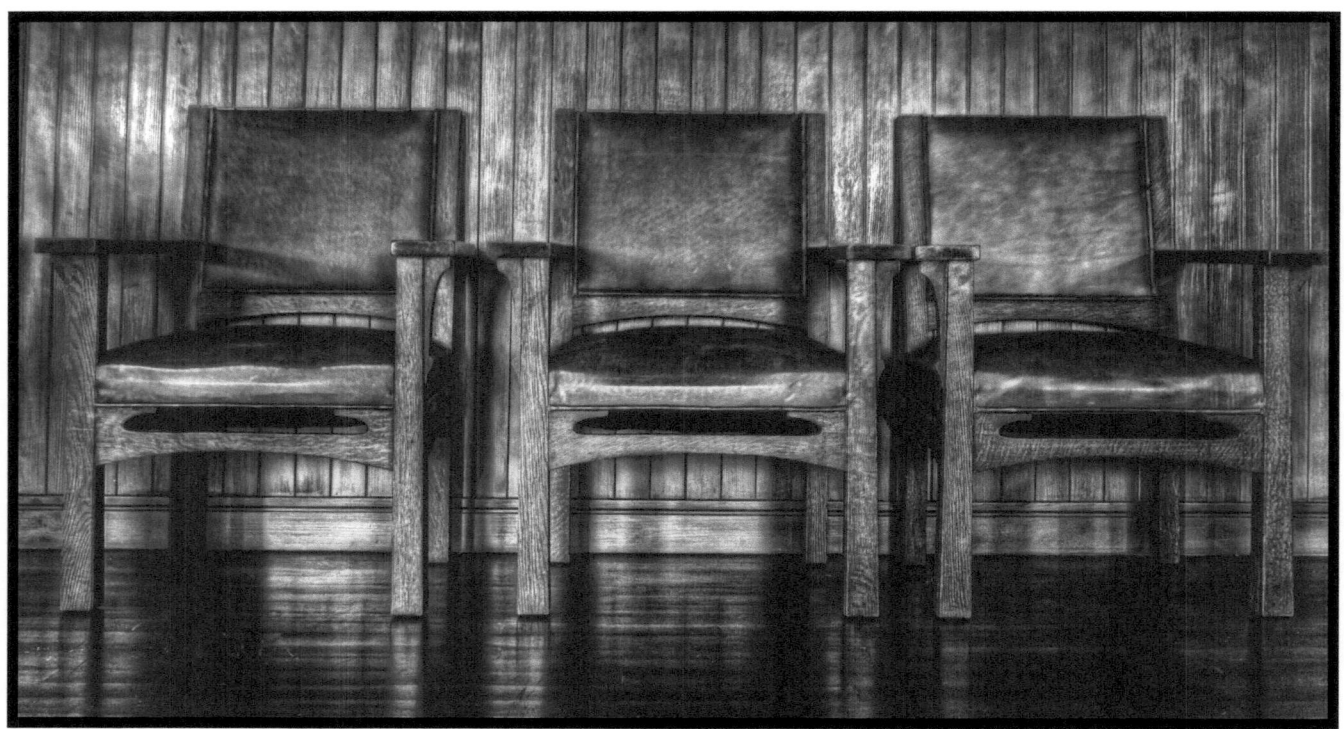

Majestic Chairs - Mel Carll

"As soon as I entered the church, the first thing I noticed was the chairs up front. You can envision the church leaders sitting proudly in front of their congregation."

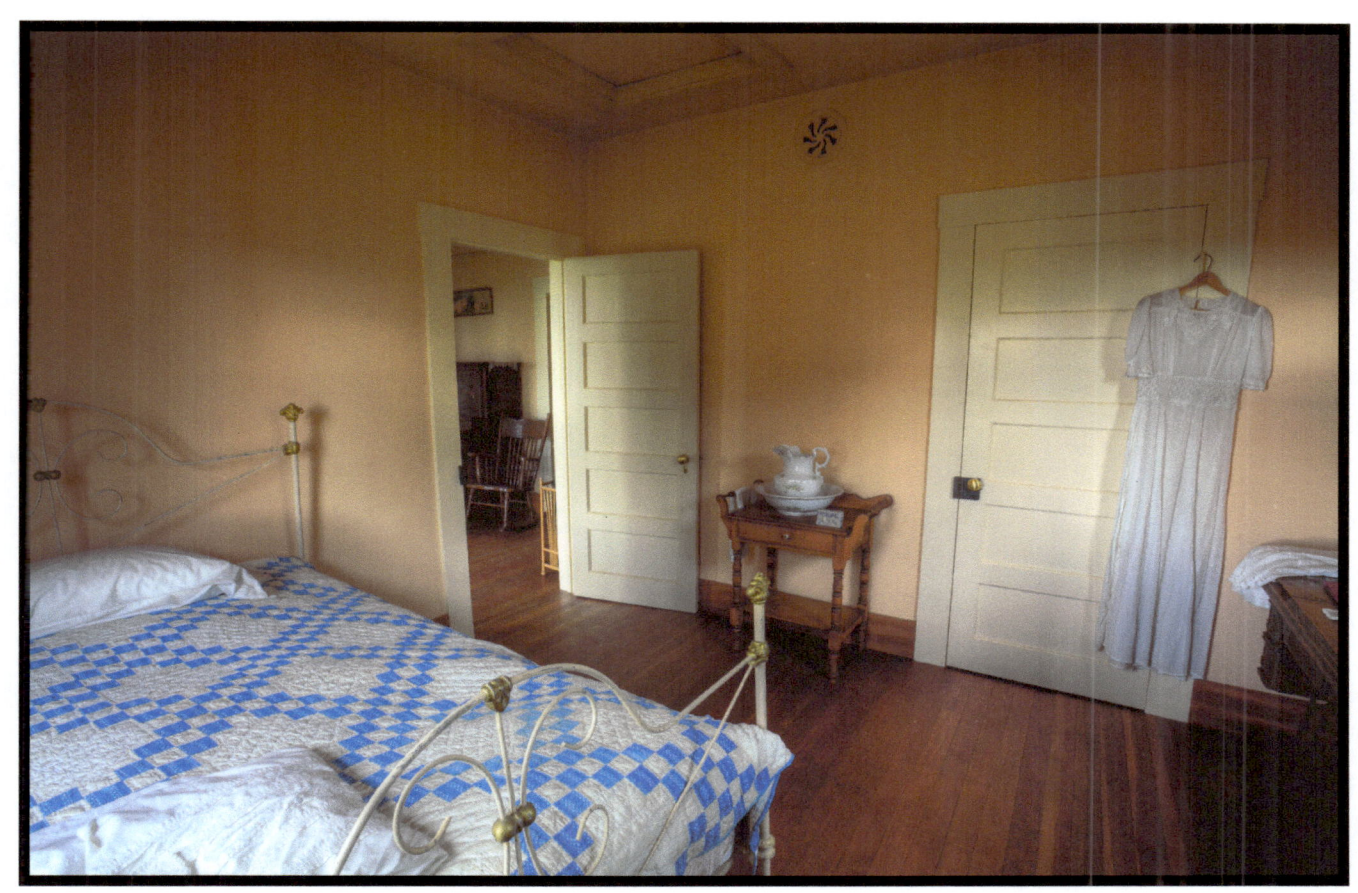

Master Bedroom - David Paul Green

'It is difficult not to compare the beautiful, yet Spartan simplicity of an Allensworth home with the belabored clut-ter of our own contemporary interior decoration. This is a bedroom in the Smith House."

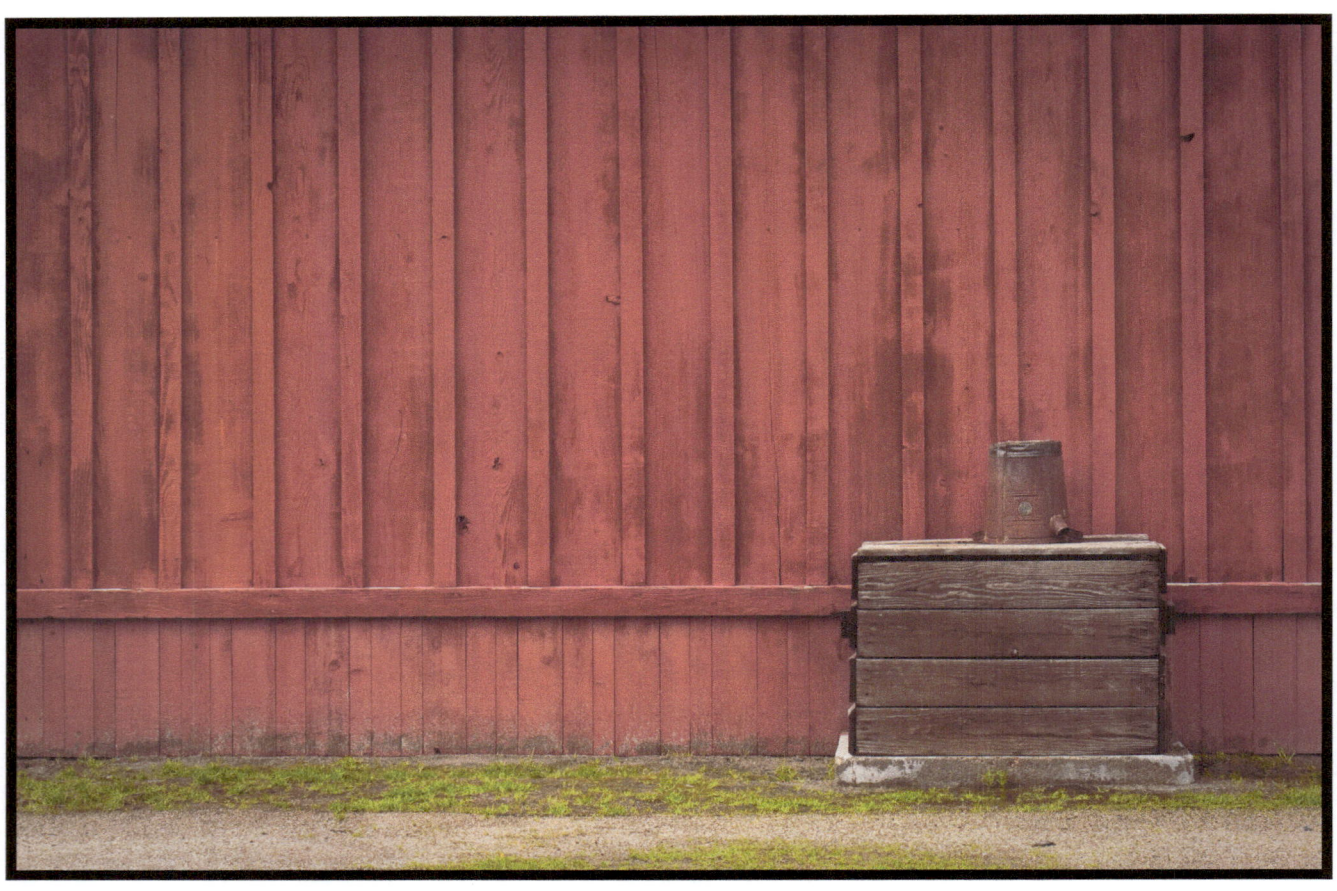

Rusted Red Pail - Clark Campbell

"Viewed from the left side of the Scott-Gross Store. The Scott-Gross Store was the main source of medicine and health care items for the town of Allensworth."

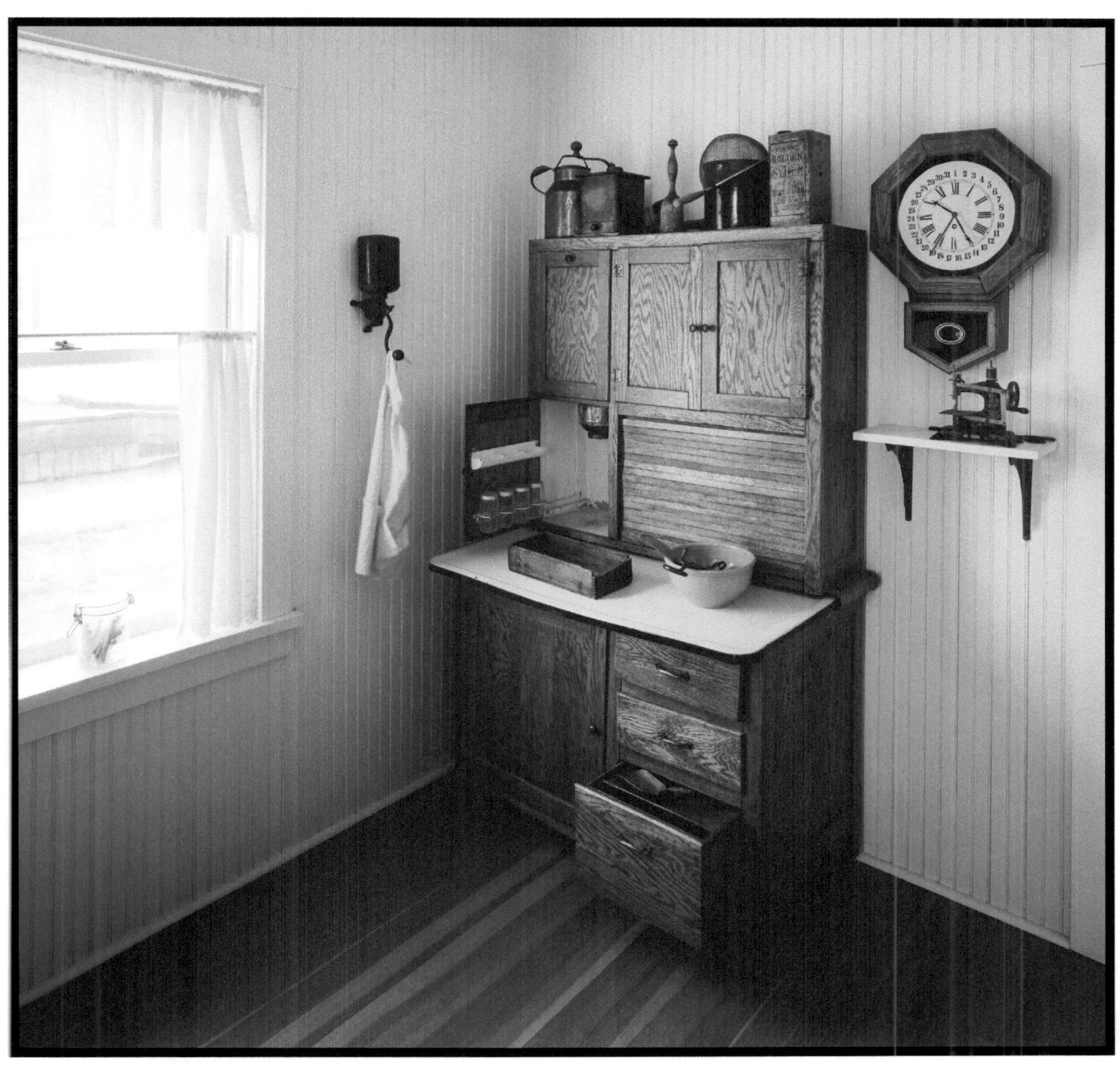

Hackett House Kitchen - Rick Russell

"Kitchen cabinet located in Hackett House."

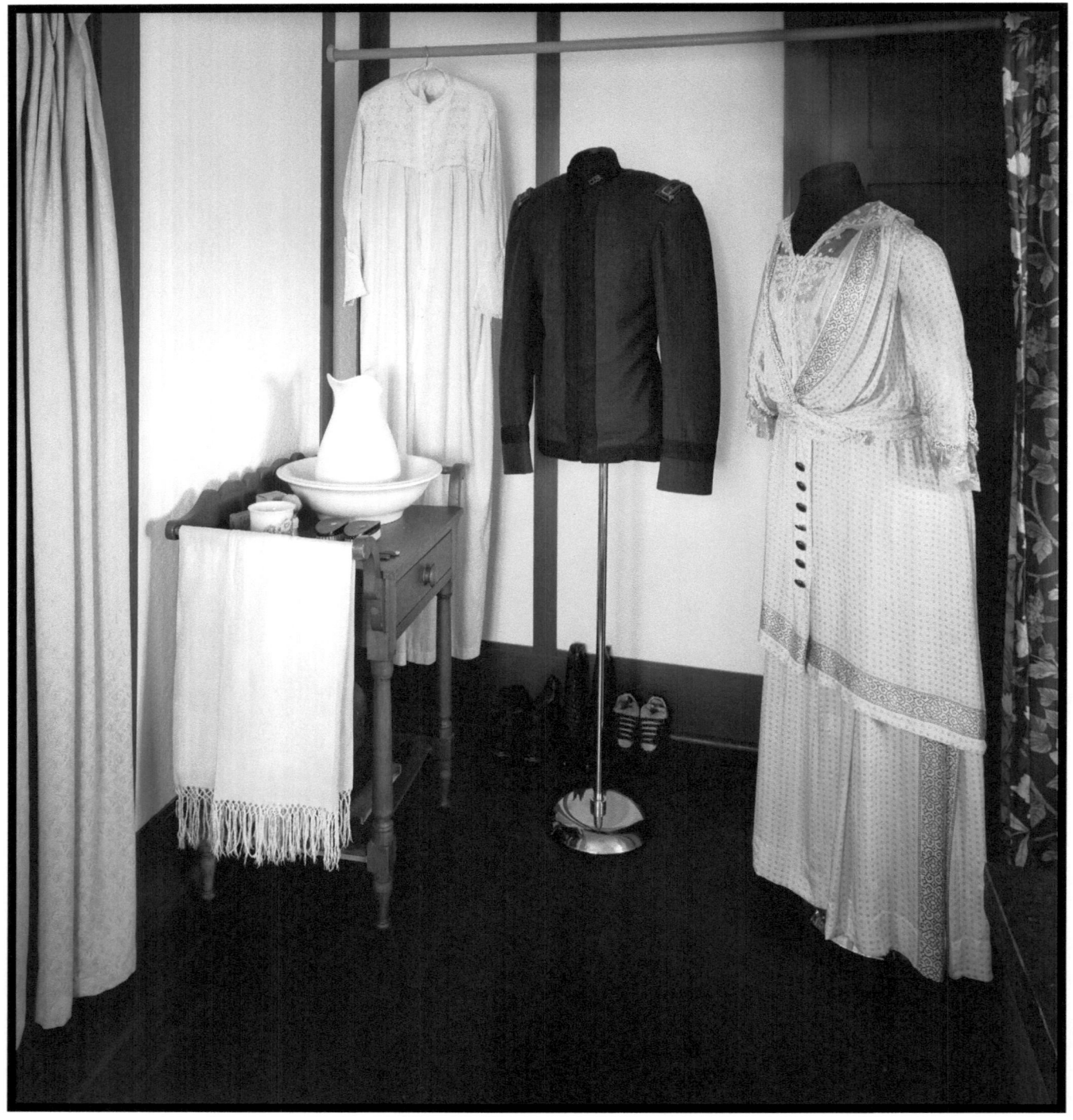

Allensworth House Closet - Rick Russell

"The tunic of Colonel Allensworth and dress of Mrs. Allensworth hung in the closet area of their bedroom."

Exhibition Checklist

A Lady's Dresser, 2010
April Bielefeldt
9 1/2 x 14"
Digital print on premium luster photographic paper
California African American Museum Collection

Kitchen Window, 2010
April Bielefeldt
14 x 9 1/2"
Digital print on premium luster photographic paper
California African American Museum Collection

Simple, 2010
April Bielefeldt
14 x 9 1/2"
Digital print on premium luster photographic paper
California African American Museum Collection

Fine Lighting, 2010
April Bielefeldt
8 x 14"
Digital print on premium luster photographic paper
California African American Museum Collection

Schoolroom, 2010
April Bielefeldt
9 1/2 x 14"
Digital print on premium luster photographic paper
California African American Museum Collection

Emmett Harden, Buffalo Soldier, Allensworth State Park, 2010
Clark Campbell
16 x 24"
Digital print on premium luster photographic paper
California African American Museum Collection

Weatherbeaten Barbershop Pole, 2010
Clark Campbell
14 x 11"
Digital print on premium luster photographic paper
California African American Museum Collection

Rusted Red Pail, 2010
Clark Campbell
9 x 14"
Digital print on premium luster photographic paper
California African American Museum Collection

Fallow Hay Rake, 2010
Clark Campbell
14 x 11"
Digital print on premium luster photographic paper
California African American Museum Collection

Blustery Nothingness, 2010
Clark Campbell
16 x 20"
Digital print on premium luster photographic paper
California African American Museum Collection

Sacred Stained Glass, 2010
Clark Campbell
9 x 14"
Digital print on premium luster photographic paper
California African American Museum Collection

Hydraulic Barbershop Footrest, 2010
Clark Campbell
14 x 11"
Digital print on premium luster photographic paper
California African American Museum Collection

Night Out, 2010
Karen Carll
24 x 16 1/2"
Digital print on premium luster photographic paper
California African American Museum Collection

Reflection, 2010
Karen Carll
9 x 14"
Digital print on premium luster photographic paper
California African American Museum Collection

Cleaning Day, 2010
Karen Carll
13 x 9"
Digital print on premium luster photographic paper
California African American Museum Collection

Wood Stove, 2010
Mel Carll
14 x 9"
Digital print on premium luster photographic paper
California African American Museum Collection

Kitchen Counter, 2010
Mel Carll
14 x 9 1/2"
Digital print on premium luster photographic paper
California African American Museum Collection

Prep Table, 2010
Mel Carll
11 x 9"
Digital print on premium luster photographic paper
California African American Museum Collection

Noble Barn on a Stormy Day, 2010
Mel Carll
24 x 14"
Digital print on premium luster photographic paper
California African American Museum Collection

Schoolhouse, 2010
Mel Carll
24 x 15 1/2"
Digital print on premium luster photographic paper
California African American Museum Collection

Majestic Chairs, 2010
Mel Carll
7 1/2 x 14"
Digital print on premium luster photographic paper
California African American Museum Collection

Old Singer, 2010
Mel Carll
7 1/2" x 14"
Digital print on premium luster photographic paper
California African American Museum Collection

Allensworth, 2010
Jean Carter
11 x 14"
Digital print on premium luster photographic paper
California African American Museum Collection

School Teacher - Amanda Moore, 2010
Jean Carter
11 x 14"
Digital print on premium luster photographic paper
California African American Museum Collection

Doll, 2010
Jean Carter
11 x 14"
Digital print on premium luster photographic paper
California African American Museum Collection

The Barbershop, 2010
Jean Carter
11 x 14"
Digital print on premium luster photographic paper
California African American Museum Collection

Girl's Undergarment, 2010
Jean Carter
11" x 14"
Digital print on premium luster photographic paper
California African American Museum Collection

Sunday Best, 2010
Jean Carter
11 x 14"
Digital print on premium luster photographic paper
California African American Museum Collection

Oliver Typewriter, 2010
Jean Carter
11 x 14"
Digital print on premium luster photographic paper
California African American Museum Collection

Fresh Eggs for Sale, 2010
Jean Carter
14 x 9"
Digital print on premium luster photographic paper
California African American Museum Collection

Allensworth Hotel, Side View, 2010
Ted Dayton
13 x 11"
Digital print on premium luster photographic paper
California African American Museum Collection

Rear View of Colonel Allensworth's Home, 2010
Ted Dayton
20 x 21"
Digital print on premium luster photographic paper
California African American Museum Collection

Front Porch of Colonel Allensworth's Home, 2010
Ted Dayton
13 x 10 1/2"
Digital print on premium luster photographic paper
California African American Museum Collection

Baptist Church, 2010
Ted Dayton
7 x 14"
Digital print on premium luster photographic paper
California African American Museum Collection

The Kitchen in Colonel Allensworth's Home, 2010
Ted Dayton
12 x 11"
Digital print on premium luster photographic paper
California African American Museum Collection

The Kitchen of Colonel Allensworth's Home, 2010
Ted Dayton
20 x 21"
Digital print on premium luster photographic paper
California African American Museum Collection

Hotel Dining Room, 2010
Ted Dayton
14 x 10 1/2"
Digital print on premium luster photographic paper
California African American Museum Collection

Stormy Reflection, 2010
David Green
9 1/2 x 14"
Digital print on premium luster photographic paper
California African American Museum Collection

Outbuildings, 2010
David Green
5 x 14"
Digital print on premium luster photographic paper
California African American Museum Collection

Smattering of Wildflowers, 2010
David Green
9 1/2 x 14"
Digital print on premium luster photographic paper
California African American Museum Collection

Master Bedroom, 2010
David Green
9 1/2 x 14"
Digital print on premium luster photographic paper
California African American Museum Collection

Kitchen Objects, 2010
David Green
9 1/2 x 14"
Digital print on premium luster photographic paper
California African American Museum Collection

Barbershop, 2010
David Green
9 1/2 x 14"
Digital print on premium luster photographic paper
California African American Museum Collection

Stormy School Day, 2010
Robert Mance
14 x 9"
Digital print on premium luster photographic paper
California African American Museum Collection

Supper Time at the Colonel Allensworth House, 2010
Robert Mance
14 x 9 1/2"
Digital print on premium luster photographic paper
California African American Museum Collection

Shoes for Sale, 2010
Robert Mance
14 x 9"
Digital print on premium luster photographic paper
California African American Museum Collection

Phillips House, 2010
20 x 13 1/2"
Robert Mance
Digital print on premium luster photographic paper
California African American Museum Collection

Barbershop Tools, 2010
Robert Mance
20 x 13 1/2"
Digital print on premium luster photographic paper
California African American Museum Collection

Barbershop Bottles, 2010
Robert Mance
11 x 12"
Digital print on premium luster photographic paper
California African American Museum Collection

Sit for a Spell, 2010
Robert Mance
14 x 9"
Digital print on premium luster photographic paper
California African American Museum Collection

Ink & Pen, 2010
Robert Mance
14 x 9 1/2"
Digital print on premium luster photographic paper
California African American Museum Collection

Standing Guard, 2010
Robert Mance
14 x 9 1/2"
Digital print on premium luster photographic paper
California African American Museum Collection

Hackett House Kitchen, 2010
Rick Russell
20 x 19"
Digital print on premium luster photographic paper
California African American Museum Collection

Alice Royal Portrait, 2010
Rick Russell
14 x 11"
Digital print on premium luster photographic paper
California African American Museum Collection

Stove in Phillips House, 2010
Rick Russell
11 x 14"
Digital print on premium luster photographic paper
California African American Museum Collection

Dodson House and Restaurant Kitchen, 2010
Rick Russell
14 x 11"
Digital print on premium luster photographic paper
California African American Museum Collection

Shelving in Milner House and Barbershop, 2010
Rick Russell
12 1/2 x 11"
Digital print on premium luster photographic paper
California African American Museum Collection

Allensworth House Closet, 2010
Rick Russell
12 x 11"
Digital print on premium luster photographic paper
California African American Museum Collection

Ground Color, 2010
Christy Stallcup
9 1/2 x 14"
Digital print on premium luster photographic paper
California African American Museum Collection

Mrs. Alice Royal, 2010
Christy Stallcup
14 x 9 1/2"
Digital print on premium luster photographic paper
California African American Museum Collection

Bowler Hat – Hindsman & Co General Store, 2010
Christy Stallcup
14 x 9 1/2"
Digital print on premium luster photographic paper
California African American Museum Collection

Full Bloom, 2010
Christy Stallcup
9 1/2 x 14"
Digital print on premium luster photographic paper
California African American Museum Collection

Phillips House, 2010
Christy Stallcup
14 x 9 1/2"
Digital print on premium luster photographic paper
California African American Museum Collection

Grave Marker – Allensworth Cemetery, 2010
Christy Stallcup
14 x 9 1/2"
Digital print on premium luster photographic paper
California African American Museum Collection

Anna Pierson – Allensworth Cemetery, 2010
Christy Stallcup
9 1/2 x 14"
Digital print on premium luster photographic paper
California African American Museum Collection

The Photographers

April Bielefeldt holds degrees in Fine Art and Fashion Design from Iowa State University. After moving to California, April was showing and selling her large acrylic paintings in Fine Art shows throughout California. Her passion has turned to leading small group photo tours of California wildflowers, California backroads, and to Maine, Vermont and New Hampshire during fall foliage season.

Digital prints • *Camera: Canon EOS 40D*

Clark Campbell's first interest in photography came while raking leaves in the backyard of his childhood home. The quick portrait he and his mother shot of themselves while burning the last frame on a roll of film piqued his passion and started him on his way. While he enjoys all types of photography, the challenge of capturing a moment with a subject during portraiture is where he finds the most creative satisfaction and is where he focuses his professional efforts today.

Digital prints • *Camera: Nikon D90*

Karen Carll is an award-winning photographer living in the Santa Clarita Valley. Although she has been taking photos off and on since she was in grade school, Karen's interest in photography was reignited when she picked up her first digital camera in 2006. Since that day she has been traveling around the country capturing the everyday wonders of the world around us, meeting great people and sharing her passion for photography with everyone!

Digital prints • *Camera: Nikon D3*

Mel Carll is a Santa Clarita Valley based photographer shooting weddings, events and corporate assignments. Mel is an award-winning photographer. He is also an instructor and his work can be seen in several publications. He is excited to bring the SCV Center for Photography in Santa Clarita to the community, assisting photographers of all levels to advance their goals and knowledge of photography.

Digital prints • *Camera: Nikon D300*

Jean Carter is an award-winning fine art photographer based in California's Santa Clarita Valley. Jean's credits include shooting stock photography for Ernst & Young. In 2006, her "snowflake" submission was chosen as one of four holiday cards featured and distributed to employees and clients world-wide. Jean states, "The work I have been able to produce for the Allensworth Project has been highly rewarding. I have been honored to work with this team of creative photographers to document this important piece of California history."

Digital prints • *Camera: Canon EOS 5D*

Ted Dayton has been a professional photographer since 1976, beginning as a studio photographer in Dallas. His career has included a half-decade on the red carpets of Hollywood and he now specializes mainly in architectural interiors and environmental portraits.

Digital prints from Ilford film • *Camera: Mamiya Pro 645*

David Green is a writer, photographer and teacher. He also plays a mean blues harp. He exposed his first frame of film on his father's Finetta 88 camera as a child. By his teens, he had a darkroom in his bedroom closet. By college, he was shooting for local newspapers and magazines. David's quest is for moments of transcendence, when beauty arises from the mundane, and both artist and audience become lost in time, then, find something unexpected.

Digital prints • *Camera: Canon EOS 5D*

Robert Mance's favorite time of day is waking up before the crack of dawn to hike to some forgotten waterfront or edge of nowhere, to greet the morning sun and the beauty that exists around him. He greets these forgotten sights with a click of his shutter; to bring home to eyes who haven't seen the beauty that exists in the world. Robert wishes not only to take the breath away of each person who views his photos, but also to inspire them to go out and see what only his eyes have seen.

Digital prints • *Camera: Canon 1DS MKII*

Rick Russell (editor) is a native Californian, has been enchanted with the art of Photography since elementary school. His first magical photographic moment took place 40 years ago in high school, when he saw a print develop in the darkroom. A traditionalist, Rick shoots film exclusively, and is in no hurry to join the digital craze. Rick's format of choice is large format, which is a slower, more deliberate form of photography. Always shooting his large format camera from a tripod, Rick photographs landscapes large and small, as well as architecture. An avid hiker and traveler, his joy of photography results in lugging pounds of camera equipment into the high Sierra and distant places to capture special places and moments.

Digital prints from Ilford Delta 100 film • *Camera: Ebony SV45U2*

Christy Stallcup began her professional career in photography in 2009. She has worked as a graphic designer and photographer for a local publication, but primarily prefers free-lance work. She specializes in event photography and school photography, and has already received several awards and gained recognition for her work.

All: Digital Prints • *Camera: Nikon D700*

Acknowledgements

My family and friends have referred to the idea for this project as being my "baby." Well, this particular baby would not have been produced with out the skill and herculean efforts of David Green in organizing the placement of photos and editing the text. Thank you David for bringing this project to life!

This project also could not have happened without the talented group of photographers, who were willing to trek to Allensworth in cold and at times rainy conditions to produce a collection of photographs which I had to sort through to come up with the photos comprising this books.

Thank you Ted Dayton, Robert Mance, Jean Carter, Christy Stallcup, Clark Campbell, Karen Carll, Mel Carll, David Green and April Bielefeldt.

The patience of Steven Ptomey and his staff of the State of California Department of Parks and Recreation at Allensworth allowed the team of photographers to do our thing.

It is the spirit embodied by the park docents, all members of the Friends of Allensworth, who inspired us all to provide the best possible creative images. Thank you to all for your assistance and support!

Finally, thank you to Mar Hollingsworth, Charmaine Jefferson, and the staff at the California African American Museum, for believing in Allensworth, and our images, and giving this project the nurturing needed to make it worthy of an exhibit.

Rick Russell is a photographer living in the Santa Clarita Valley. He specializes in large-format film photography.

Project Credits

Rick Russell — Editor, Producer
David Green, Monteverdi Creative Inc. — Book Design & Layout
Mel Carll, SCV Center for Photography — Exhibit Printmaking
Dusty Stiles — Exhibit Video and Editing

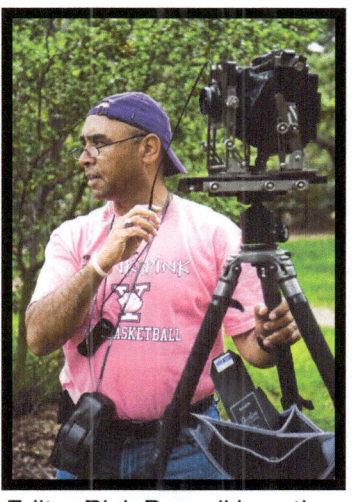

Editor Rick Russell in action.

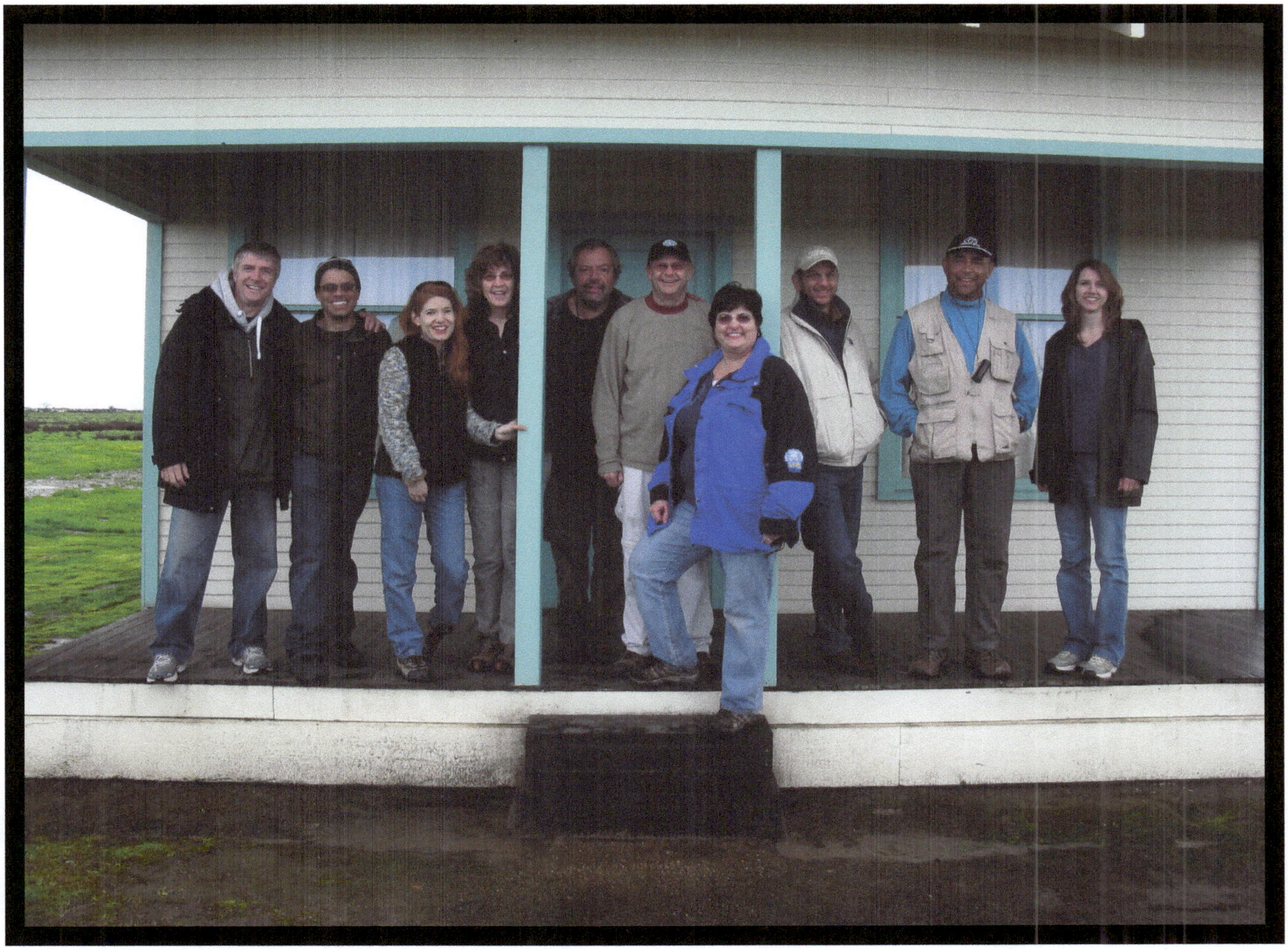

The Project Team
(left to right) Clark Campbell, David Green, April Bielfeldt, Karen Carll, Robert Mance, Mel Carll, Jean Carter, Ted Dayton, Rick Russell, Christy Stallcup

www.ingramcontent.com/pod-product-compliance
Lightning Source LLC
Chambersburg PA
CBHW050736180526
45159CB00003B/1245